The Writings of
Henry D. Thoreau

The Higher Law

HENRY D. THOREAU

The Higher Law

THOREAU ON CIVIL DISOBEDIENCE AND REFORM

EDITED BY WENDELL GLICK

WITH AN INTRODUCTION BY HOWARD ZINN

PRINCETON UNIVERSITY PRESS

PRINCETON AND OXFORD

*Editorial expenses for this volume have been met in part
by grants from the National Endowment for the Humanities
administered through the Center for Editions of
American Authors of the Modern Language Association.*

*This paperback was originally published in hardcover in 1973
under the title* Reform Papers *by Princeton University Press*

Library of Congress Control Number 2004100971

ISBN 0-691-11876-0

British Library Cataloging-in-Publication Data is available

Printed on acid-free paper. ∞

pup.princeton.edu

Printed in the United States of America

10   9   8   7   6   5   4   3   2   1

Editorial Board

The Writings

Contents

Introduction

IN THE YEAR 1968 I was called to Milwaukee to tes-
tify in the case of the Milwaukee Fourteen, a group of
priests, nuns, and laypeople who had gone into a draft
board, taken thousands of its documents, and burned
them in a symbolic protest against the war in Vietnam.
As a historian of social movements, I was asked to discuss the role of civil disobedience in American history.
The judge was clearly uneasy, but he allowed me to
answer the question. I spoke of the principles of the
Declaration of Independence, and of its insistence that
when a government becomes destructive of basic
human rights, it is the duty of the people to "alter or
abolish it." I began to talk about Henry David Thoreau
and his decision to break the law in protest against the
U.S. invasion of Mexico in 1846. At this point, Judge
Larsen interrupted. He pounded his gavel and said:
"You can't discuss that. That is getting to the heart of
the matter."

You will find in this volume (published previously in
hardcover as *Reform Papers*) what are usually called
the "political writings" of Thoreau. Indeed, he is deal-
ing here with the incendiary issues of his time: the
Mexican War, the Fugitive Slave Act, the execution of
John Brown. The term "political," however, does not do
justice to the breadth and depth of Thoreau's ideas. He
looks beyond the immediate subjects of contention to
ask the fundamental questions pondered before and
after his time by the world's great thinkers: Plato,
Machiavelli, Hobbes, Locke, Rousseau, Marx, Tolstoy.
That is, he addresses the obligations of the citizen to
government, of law to justice, of human beings to one
another.

In this collection, he does something more—he asks the most troubling question of human existence: how shall we live our lives in a society that makes being human more and more difficult?

The words of Thoreau on all these issues, written a century and a half ago, resound loud with meaning as I write this at the end of the year 2003. The nation is at war, as it was when Thoreau declared his resistance to government. This time, however, it is not a finite war, limited in time and space, but what seems an endless war, or series of wars, because the enemy has been declared to be "terrorism," which cannot be confined to one place, or one time. All that Thoreau wrote so long ago speaks to us today and makes us wonder about our responsibility as citizens, as human beings.

It is well known that Thoreau spent a night in jail, in the summer of 1846, because he refused to pay his taxes in protest against the war with Mexico. It may be useful, then, to take a close look at that war, to help us understand his action, his thinking.

Mexico, which had won its independence in a revolutionary war against Spain, was at that time much larger than it is today. It included what are now the states of Texas, New Mexico, Utah, Nevada, Arizona, California, and part of Colorado. In the year 1836, Texas, aided by the United States, declared its independence from Mexico, calling itself the "Lone Star Republic." It was brought into the Union as a state by act of Congress in 1845, and various influential newspapers and politicians became excited about the prospect of expanding westward into Mexican territory. John O'Sullivan, editor of the *Democratic Review,* wrote that it was the nation's "manifest destiny to overspread the continent allotted by Providence for the free development of our yearly multiplying millions." The phrase took hold: Manifest Destiny.

The following year, President James Polk, who on the night of his inauguration had confided to his secretary of the navy that he was determined to acquire California, sent troops to the southern border of Texas, as far as the Rio Grande River, into territory claimed by Mexico, historically inhabited by Mexicans. A clash between Mexican and U.S. troops followed, and a U.S. patrol was virtually wiped out. Even before this incident, a U.S. colonel on the southern front, Ethan Allen Hitchcock, a reader of Shakespeare, Chaucer, Hegel, and Spinoza, wrote in his diary: "I have said from the first that the United States are the aggressors. . . . It looks as if the government sent a small force on purpose to bring on war, so as to have a pretext for taking California and as much of this country as it chooses."

President Polk falsely claimed that Mexico had invaded the United States and asked Congress for a declaration of war. The Whig Party was presumably against slavery and against the war, but they were not against expansion, and they saw the acquisition of California as commercially valuable. Thus they voted overwhelmingly with the Democrats in Congress in favor of war. It was an early manifestation of the historic unity of both major parties in acquiescing in a presidential decision for war.

The war with Mexico intensified the bitter controversy already simmering in the United States over slavery. Ralph Waldo Emerson had predicted that "the United States will conquer Mexico, but it will be as the man swallows the arsenic, which brings him down in turn. Mexico will poison us." Commenting on Emerson's warning, the Civil War historian James McPherson has written: "He was right. The poison was slavery." Opposition to the war by the growing antislavery movement was based on the fear that the new territories would expand the area of slavery in the country.

The poet James Russell Lowell had his character Hosea Biglow say:

> "They jest want this Californy
> So's to lug new slave-states in
> To abuse ye, an' to scorn ye,
> An' to plunder ye like sin."

Thoreau lived in Concord, twenty miles from Boston, which was becoming a center of antislavery agitation. He graduated from Harvard in 1837. Six years earlier, on January 1, 1831, William Lloyd Garrison had launched the first issue of the antislavery newspaper *The Liberator*, declaring of slavery, "On this subject I do not wish to think or speak or write with moderation. No! No! Tell a man whose house is on fire to give a moderate alarm."

All about Thoreau there were ardent opponents of slavery, including his mother and sisters. Ralph Waldo Emerson was a friend and mentor, and the two of them joined forces, over the objection of conservative curators of the Concord Lyceum, to invite the fiery abolitionist orator Wendell Phillips to speak. Thoreau's review of Phillips's speech, and of his character, is included in this volume ("Wendell Phillips Before Concord Lyceum"). You will also find in this volume Thoreau's 1844 *Dial* article in praise of Nathaniel Rogers, editor of the New Hampshire abolitionist newspaper *Herald of Freedom*, who had written: "Slavery must be cried down, denounced down, ridiculed down."

For six years before the Mexican War, in order to protest a government that countenanced slavery, Thoreau had not paid his poll tax. But in the summer of 1846, in the midst of his two-year stay at Walden Pond to write *A Week on the Concord and Merrimack Rivers* and to commune alone with nature, he ventured into Concord to join a huckleberry-picking party. There, he encountered the local constable, who asked him to pay his tax. He refused and was taken to the town jail. That night, as he lay awake in his cell, the ideas began to form about how an individual should behave in relation to the government. The next day he was told that someone had appeared to pay his tax (he never found out whether it was his friend Emerson or one of his aunts), and he reluctantly left the jail, to return to the huckleberry field.

The Mexican War ended in 1848 with the United States taking two-fifths of Mexican territory. But before it ended, there were protests against the war going far beyond Thoreau's mild act. The battle deaths and mutilations were not the only horrors of the war. A regimental surgeon of the Second Regiment of Mississippi Rifles saw his regiment packed into the holds of transports and reported on what he saw and heard: "The wild screams of the delirious, the lamentations of the sick, and the melancholy groans of the dying." More than nine thousand soldiers deserted. There were mutinies against officers, resentment against the caste system. One Pennsylvania volunteer wrote: "Some of our officers are very good men but the balance of them are very tyrannical and brutal. . . . A soldier's life is very disgusting." On the road to Mexico City seven of General Winfield Scott's eleven regiments, their enlistment times up, faded away. The Massachusetts Volunteers, returning home with half their 630 men dead, honored with a dinner, hissed their commanding general.

Thoreau had left his cabin at Walden Pond in the fall of 1847. A lecture that he gave soon after at the Concord Lyceum was called "The Rights and Duties of the Individual in Relation to Government." He kept refining it, and it appeared in print in the spring of

1849 as "Resistance to Civil Government." The title "Civil Disobedience" was used in the printing of the essay in 1866, four years after Thoreau's death; the title may or may not have been Thoreau's. Authorial or not, it has become the standard title, the one by which millions have known the essay.

How shall we define civil disobedience so that we may have a common ground for discussing it? I will define it as the deliberate violation of a law in pursuit of some social goal. Thus Thoreau's act of nonpayment of taxes fits that definition, his goal to make some small statement against war, against slavery. Gandhi's marches in violation of British law had as their aim unseating British rule in India. The African American students who in 1960 "sat in" at lunch counters to protest racial segregation were violating local law, and even federal law, since the Supreme Court had not given constitutional approval to desegregation in private businesses.

At the center of Thoreau's great essay (though he doesn't make the reference) is that stunning idea expressed in the Declaration of Independence: governments are artificial creations, set up to serve the interests of the people. That idea was soon overwhelmed by the reality of the Constitution and the establishment of an actual government. Now a small group of powerful men could use the government to advance their own interests, to make war, to compromise with slavery. But why should people of conscience defer to such a government and its laws? Why should they not exercise their own moral judgment? When a government supports evil, it is the duty of its citizens to withhold their support from the government, to resist its demands.

The early 1850s saw a series of militant acts of civil disobedience, in violation of the Fugitive Slave Act. There is no evidence of anyone's referring to Thoreau, but clearly the idea of resistance to unjust laws was being put into effect. The passage of the Fugitive Slave Act in 1850 was part of a package of provisions in what was called the Compromise of 1850, designed to satisfy both sides of the slavery dispute. California was admitted to the Union as a nonslave state, but to appease the South, federal marshals were required to help slave owners recapture their escaped slaves and were fined $1,000 if they refused. Federal commissioners were to decide whether in fact a black person was an escaped slave; they were paid $10 if they decided in favor of the slave owner, $5 if in favor of the slave. During that decade of the 1850s, federal commissioners returned 332 blacks to slavery and declared free only 11. There was no statute of limitations: one black man in southern Indiana was apprehended, in front of his wife and children, and returned to a slaveholder who said he had run away nineteen years before.

Almost as soon as the act went into effect and the first escaped slaves were apprehended, Northern abolitionists, black and white, set out to obstruct the law. A slave owner in Georgia sent two agents to recapture William and Ellen Craft, a husband and wife who had escaped slavery two years earlier and were now living in Boston, a center of abolitionism. Blacks and whites joined to protect the Crafts. Wendell Phillips declared: "We must trample this law under our feet." The law, said the local antislavery society, "is to be denounced, resisted, and disobeyed." The slave-catchers were warned that they were not safe in Boston, and they returned to Georgia. William and Ellen Craft were put on a ship to England.

President Millard Fillmore threatened to send federal troops to enforce the Fugitive Slave Act, but the abolitionists defied him. The Reverend Theodore Parker, an abolitionist whose parish the Crafts had joined, wrote to Fillmore: "I would rather lie all my life in jail, and starve there, than refuse to protect one of these parishioners of mine. . . . I must reverence the laws of God, come of that what will come."

There were more acts of defiance against the Fugitive Slave Act. A black man named Shadrach Minkins, who had escaped from Virginia and was working as a waiter in a Boston coffeehouse, was captured by agents and taken to a federal courthouse. A group of black men broke into the courtroom, rescued Minkins, and put him on the Underground Railroad to Canada. Eight of the rescuers, four black and four white, were indicted by a federal grand jury. But when they went to trial, juries refused to convict them.

In Christiana, Pennsylvania, a shoot-out took place over the attempt of a slave owner and federal marshals to return two black men to slavery. Two dozen black men protected the fugitives, and the slave owner was killed. President Fillmore called on the marines, who, with federal marshals, searched the countryside and arrested more than thirty black men and a half-dozen whites. They were indicted, but the jury acquitted the first defendant and the government dropped the remaining cases.

Thoreau's essay "Slavery in Massachusetts," reprinted in this volume, was drawn from journal entries of 1851 and 1854, and appeared in part in Garrison's *The Liberator*. That essay has been overshadowed by his more famous one on civil disobedience, but it deserves close attention. He was provoked by an incident in 1854, when President Franklin Pierce dispatched federal troops, joined by state militia and local police, to capture Anthony Burns, a slave escaped from Virginia. Black and white abolitionists used a battering ram against the courthouse doors but were repulsed. Burns was marched to the waterfront, through streets lined with his supporters, to the sound of church bells tolling, and sent back to slavery.

In his essay, Thoreau plays on a theme that recurs in the essays in this volume: the complicity of the government and the courts, the silence of citizens in the face of that collusion ("I am surprised to see men going about their business as if nothing had happened"), and the cowardice of the press. Thoreau does not expect the government to act in the interests of justice and believes that in the long run this will be widely recognized: "A government which deliberately enacts injustice, and persists in it, will at length ever become the laughing-stock of the world." One cannot help recalling that when the United States made war in Vietnam in the 1960s, it drew the opposition of people all over the world, and that when it was on the verge of invading Iraq in 2003, ten million people in fifty countries around the world protested on a single day.

Much as he reviles the government ("useless, or worse than useless") and the soldier who serves the slave master ("a fool made conspicuous by a painted coat"), Thoreau has not much hope for them. But he expects more from citizens and so is bitter about their silence when a fugitive slave, Thomas Sims, is returned forcibly to slavery in 1851. He notes that the people of Concord—on the anniversary of the shot heard round the world in 1775 and just a week after the rendition of Sims—rang the liberty bells and fired the cannons. But "when the sound of the bells died away, their liberty died away also." That could be a commentary on any celebration in the midst of war.

Thoreau has no respect for the law when the law allows war and protects slavery, nor for the justices of the Supreme Court, as they, obedient to the Constitution, affirm the legality of holding three million people as slaves. "The law will never make men

xviii   INTRODUCTION

free; it is men who have got to make the law free."
Such judges do not ask what the murderers' tools are
for; they only inspect them to see whether they are "in
working order." Such judges do not ask "whether the
Fugitive Slave Law is right, but whether it is what they
call *constitutional*."

In "Slavery in Massachusetts" Thoreau wrote: "What
is wanted is men, not of policy, but of probity—who
recognize a higher law than the Constitution, or the
decision of the majority." (The title of the present volume is taken from this quotation.) Thoreau's attitude
toward law and toward the Constitution points very
directly to the legal controversies of our own time,
when certain Supreme Court justices and legal scholars insist their job is to decide what the Founding
Fathers meant by the words they wrote in 1787.
Thoreau asks why, in deciding moral questions, we
must ask whether "your grandfather, seventy years
ago" entered into an agreement "to serve the devil" and
therefore you must abide by that agreement, regardless
of its human consequences.

Thoreau could have been speaking about Justice Abe
Fortas, who joined the Supreme Court majority in the
spring of 1968 to uphold the conviction of a young man
who had publicly burned his draft card to protest the
war in Vietnam (a petty act of arson, one might say,
compared to William Lloyd Garrison's setting fire to
the Constitution in 1835). The court was not concerned
with whether the war was right (or even whether it was
constitutional) but considered only whether O'Brien
had violated the Conscription Act.

That same year, in an essay on civil disobedience,
Fortas wrote: "Thoreau was an inspiring figure and a
great writer; but his essay should not be read as a hand-
book on political science." His notion of "political science" clearly did not include moral philosophy but

made the former a register of whatever regulations the politicians of the time might order.

In "Slavery in Massachusetts," Thoreau is scathing about the press. The newspaper, he said "is a Bible which we read every morning and every afternoon, standing and sitting, riding and walking." Editors, he said, by their acceptance of the Fugitive Slave Act, "live and rule only by their own servility." Speaking of a certain Boston newspaper and its response when Thomas Sims was carried off to slavery, he wrote: "I have heard the gurgling of the sewer through every column."

What would Thoreau say if he were alive today? In our time, too, the press (much of it controlled by huge financial conglomerates) is largely subservient to government, especially in time of war, when a fervid nationalism distorts reportage, and criticism of government policy is often seen as unpatriotic. According to Daniel Hallin's careful study, *The "Uncensored War": The Media and Vietnam,* television coverage throughout the Vietnam War was "lopsidedly favorable to American policy in Vietnam," even more so than what he called the "remarkably docile print media."

In the second Gulf War of 2003, the major television channels rushed to declare their support of the war. The Fox News Channel regularly showed the Stars and Stripes in the upper-left-hand corner of the screen, and the words "War on Terrorism" blended into "Operation Iraqi Freedom." According to a study by Fairness and Accuracy in Reporting, even though at the moment of military victory 27 percent of the public remained opposed to the war, less than 3 percent of Americans interviewed on the major television networks were antiwar.

What Thoreau saw as a coldness in government and press toward the black slave, an abysmal failure of compassion for the "other," persisted for a hundred years, even after the end of slavery, in the continued sub-ordination of black people in this country. To white Americans they were shadowy presences, unknown as human beings.

Thoreau saw the national and local governments of his time collaborating with slavery. Until the 1960s, we saw the national government acquiescing in racial segregation, indeed in the violation of the Fourteenth and Fifteenth Amendments to the Constitution. Only when black people in the South pushed themselves into view, brought public attention by acts of civil disobe-dience, did government finally respond.

The invisibility of the "other" carries over into war, where the "enemy" is other than human and need not be considered when the casualties are counted up. Nowhere was this revealed more starkly than when atomic bombs were dropped on Hiroshima and Nagasaki. The incineration and radiation of several hundred thousand Japanese could be accepted by Americans because they were not seen as human beings, not made visible as were the victims of Japan in the Bataan Death March or, some time after the fact, the victims of Hitler in the death camps.

Similarly, the Vietnamese who died or were maimed or burned by napalm in the ferocious bombing of their country (more bombs were dropped there than in all of World War II) were not visible to Americans for many years. Their deaths were recorded as statistics, but they did not appear as human beings until the first photos of the My Lai massacre appeared a year after it was first reported in 1968.

When the first Gulf War ended in 1991, General Colin Powell reported proudly that the United States had suffered only several hundred casualties. When a reporter asked him about Iraqi casualties, Powell replied: "That is really not a matter I am terribly inter-ested in." The narrow nationalism that permitted such callousness would have troubled Thoreau deeply. "I would remind my countrymen, that they are to be men first, and Americans only at a late and convenient hour."

Civil disobedience is inherently antinationalist because it is based on a refusal to accept as an absolute the legitimacy of government; it considers the powers of government subordinate to human rights. The implication is that these rights belong to all human beings, not just those of one's own country. Black slaves were not quite of the United States. Indeed, they had been denied citizenship by the decision of the Supreme Court in the Dred Scott case of 1857. Yet Thoreau declared their rights to be above the law of the nation, even above the highest law of the nation—the Constitution.

Thoreau's essay propounded such a universal principle of human rights that it continues to be an inspiration for dissident thinkers and activists around the world. Tolstoy took note of "the savage Spanish-American war" and wrote of a "second war" waged against the government, its powerful weapon being "the obedience of every man to his own reason and conscience." Tolstoy wrote: "This, indeed, is so simple, so indubitable, and binding upon every man. 'You wish to make me a participator in murder; you demand of me money for the preparation of weapons; and want me to take part in the organized assembly of murderers' says the reasonable man—he who had neither sold nor obscured his conscience. 'But I profess that law—the same that is also professed by you—which long ago forbade not murder only, but all hostility, also, and therefore I cannot obey you.'"

Gandhi knew of both Thoreau and Tolstoy. Thoreau, he wrote, "has left a masterly treatise on the Duty of Civil Disobedience." The influence can be seen in the campaigns Gandhi organized to protest British rule in

India. In 1919 the British passed the Rowlatt Act
(remarkably similar to the "Patriot Act" passed by
Congress in 2001) which provided for preventive detention, the arrest and confinement of persons who were
"suspected of subversive activities." Persons considered "dangerous" could be detained indefinitely.
Gandhi and his followers took a pledge: "We solemnly
affirm that . . . we shall refuse civilly to obey these
laws." In 1930 Gandhi and others participated in a
civil disobedience movement against the government
monopoly on salt and the oppressive salt tax. They
marched from Ahmedabad to the beach at Dandi and
prepared salt from the sea, thus violating the salt laws.
Gandhi was arrested, but the civil disobedience continued for a year, in the course of which salt depots were
occupied, and protesters were met with brutal police
attacks.

In the United States social movements throughout
the twentieth century and into the twenty-first repeat-
edly put moral principles ahead of the law. Thoreau
had written, "Must the citizen ever for a moment, or in
the least degree, resign his conscience to the legislator? Why has every man a conscience, then? . . . It is
not desirable to cultivate a respect for the law, so much
as for the right."

In this spirit, labor organizers in the Industrial
Workers of the World went to jail again and again in
defiance of local laws. On the eve of World War I,
women picketed in the nation's capital in violation of
local ordinances and were arrested for demanding the
right to vote. In 1936 and 1937 workers in auto and rubber plants staged sit-down strikes to get recognition for
their unions.

In the 1950s and 1960s, black people in the South
carried out hundreds of acts of civil disobedience,
refusing to obey the laws mandating racial segregation,

defying the laws of trespass, disobeying the orders of police. Thoreau had written: "I quietly declare war with the State, after my fashion." Black people in the South had concluded that the U.S. government would not defend their constitutional rights under the Fourteenth and Fifteenth Amendments, and they would take action themselves.

A white city librarian in Montgomery, Alabama, wrote a letter to the Montgomery *Advertiser*, saying admiringly that the black people boycotting the city buses that winter of 1955 "had taken a lesson from Gandhi, and from our own Thoreau, who influenced Gandhi." The young seminary student John Lewis, who was beaten senseless in the attempted protest march in 1965 from Selma to Montgomery, had studied Gandhi and Thoreau.

No one brought alive the idea of civil disobedience in the United States more than Martin Luther King, Jr. He was a student of philosophy and religion, and was very aware of Thoreau and Gandhi, and no doubt their powerful ideas reinforced his own thinking. But it was the reality of racial segregation that led him and the thousands of others in the Southern movement—the sit-inners, the Freedom Riders, the marchers and picketers—to defy the law again and again.

In King's famous "Letter from Birmingham City Jail," he distinguishes between "just and unjust laws" in the way that Thoreau had distinguished between taxes he was willing to pay because they went for constructive public purposes, and taxes he would not pay because they supported a government at war. King had been arrested for violating a court injunction against demonstrations. "An unjust law," he said, "is out of harmony with the moral law."

The practice of civil disobedience was carried over from the protests against racial segregation to the movement against the war in Vietnam. Indeed, among the first to resist the draft (and to receive especially heavy prison sentences) were young black men in the South. In mid-1965, as the war in Vietnam began escalating rapidly, blacks in McComb, Mississippi, who had just learned that a classmate had been killed in Vietnam, distributed a leaflet: "No Mississippi Negroes should be fighting in Vietnam for the White man's freedom, until all the Negro People are free in Mississippi. Negro boys should not honor the draft here in Mississippi. Mothers should encourage their sons not to go."

One of the most dramatic instances of civil disobedience against the war was that of the heavyweight champion Muhammad Ali, who refused to serve in what he called a "white man's war." As punishment, boxing authorities took away his title as champion.

At no time in American history was there such a succession of acts of civil disobedience as during the war in Vietnam. Young men burned their draft cards or turned them in to the government. They refused to be inducted into the armed forces, 34,000 of them by the end of 1969. Hundreds of thousands, without public refusals, did not register for the draft.

Americans were deeply offended by these actions and argued that citizens should express themselves by going through legal channels, by voting. But Thoreau had no faith that government officials would act morally: "most legislators, politicians, lawyers, ministers, and office-holders, serve the State chiefly with their heads; and, as they rarely make any moral distinctions, they are as likely to serve the devil, without intending it, as God." He was disdainful of voting and other orthodox remedies. "They take too much time, and a man's life will be gone."

That spirit animated the priests, nuns, and laypeople who throughout the war in Vietnam broke into draft boards, seized draft records, and destroyed them to dramatize their protest against the war. When the Catonsville Nine went into a draft board office in Maryland, removed records, and set them afire with homemade napalm in the presence of reporters and onlookers, one of them, the priest and poet Daniel Berrigan, delivered a meditation: "Our apologies, good friends, for the fracture of good order, the burning of paper instead of children." In one of the many trials that followed, that of the Milwaukee Fourteen, a priest named Bob Cunnane told the court that he had tried to go through legal channels to help stop the war, that he had visited his senator and was told that people in Congress were helpless. That decided him on an action more forceful, even if it meant breaking the law and going to prison.

Disobedience spread to the armed forces. One West Point graduate, early in the war, refused to board an aircraft that would take him to a remote Vietnamese village. Three army privates refused to embark for Vietnam, denouncing the war as "immoral, illegal, and unjust"; they were court-martialed and imprisoned. An army doctor refused to teach Green Berets, a Special Forces elite, saying they were "murderers of women and children."

Tens of thousands deserted from the military, going to Canada or to Western Europe. During the fierce bombings of Hanoi and Haiphong, in December 1972, B-52 pilots refused to go on missions. Earlier that year, 50 out of 142 GIs in one company refused to go out on patrol.

After the war in Vietnam ended in 1975, a determined group of pacifists continued to protest the militarization of the country, the buildup of nuclear weapons, by acts of civil disobedience. Beginning in 1980 with a group called the Plowshares Eight (taking their name from the biblical injunction to beat swords into plowshares), they invaded nuclear facilities, committing small symbolic acts of sabotage. In the next twenty-three years at least seventy-five similar actions were carried out, almost always resulting in jail sentences.

Although it was supported by most Americans, the first Gulf War in 1991 led to mass demonstrations of protest in American cities, as well as to refusals of military service by young men and women. A physician named Lynda Reiser, explaining why she would defy the order sending her to Iraq, wrote: "I object to participation in war in any form. I believe in the preservation of life at all costs. . . . I cannot participate in war, either as a combatant or as a non-combatant, because my doing so would represent my agreement with war."

This is exactly what Thoreau advocated in the face of evils like slavery or war, that people should withdraw their support from the government. It is not enough to hold an opinion, he said. One must act. "When the subject has refused allegiance, and the officer has resigned his office, then the revolution is accomplished."

Thoreau's next sentences are disquieting and make it clear he is not an absolute pacifist. "But even suppose blood should flow. Is there not a sort of blood shed when the conscience is wounded?" He seems to have accepted that an evil as gross as slavery—the captivity of three million people—could not be overcome without some degree of violence.

John Brown's life epitomized the belief that violence would be necessary to abolish slavery. With a small band of like-minded men, he went to Kansas, which had become a battleground between pro- and antislavery forces. There were killings on both sides, and at one point Brown and his men carried out a nighttime raid on a pro-slavery settlement and killed five people in cold blood.

Thoreau delivered to the citizens of Concord his lecture "A Plea for Captain John Brown" twelve days after Brown, with his sons and a small group of white and black abolitionists, tried to seize the federal arsenal at Harper's Ferry, Virginia. Their aim was to incite a general slave revolt, but the plan miscarried, they were captured, and Brown lay wounded, awaiting trial.

Thoreau's passionate talk is not a defense of John Brown but, as he titled it, a plea, an expression of sympathy and admiration. It is very unlikely that Thoreau would have participated in the kind of action Brown had engaged in, yet he defended Brown's "right to interfere by force with the slaveholder, in order to rescue the slave." Brown's firearms, he said, "were employed in a righteous cause."

Emerson, with a similar passion, said of John Brown that "he will make the gallows glorious like the cross." Emerson and Thoreau were both outraged at the rush by both the state of Virginia and the national government to execute Brown, and the "cold-blooded way," as Thoreau put it, that newspaper editors and others, even abolitionists, talked of the man as "dangerous" and "insane." Shortly after John Brown was hanged for killing people, believing he was advancing the cause of freedom for slaves, the U.S. government engaged in a war, presumably to abolish slavery, and 600,000 died on the battlefields. Would any one dare to refer to the U.S. government as "dangerous" and "insane"?

Running through Thoreau's essay about John Brown is a powerful theme that speaks to our own time: the hypocrisy of government officials who put to death those who have killed one, two, or ten persons, all with an air of righteousness, buttressed by the law, but who themselves plan and carry out wars in which millions die.

"War is peace" was the slogan of the Big Brother state described in George Orwell's novel *1984*. We carry out wars in the name of peace. In the United States we keep two million people in prison in the name of order. Thoreau's words speak directly to our time: "We preserve the so-called 'peace' of our community by deeds of petty violence every day. Look at the policeman's billy and hand cuffs! Look at the jail! Look at the gallows!"

We are speaking not of totalitarian governments but of governments that call themselves democracies as does ours. We pride ourselves on having representative government. But, as Thoreau says, still speaking of John Brown, "what a monster of a government is that where the noblest faculties of the mind, and the *whole* heart, are not *represented*."

Thoreau's great insight was that there is a moral emptiness in government unless it is filled by the actions of citizens on behalf of justice. That corresponds exactly to the democratic philosophy of the Declaration of Independence, in which governments have no inherent right to exist or to rule, but deserve to do so only when they fulfill the charge given them by the people: to protect everyone's equal right to "life, liberty, and the pursuit of happiness."

In our time, that philosophy is realized in the actions of those who, in defiance of government, in defiance of laws they consider supportive of war and injustice, carry out acts of civil disobedience. That might mean damaging weapons of war, or refusing to pay taxes to support a huge military budget, or refusing to join a military campaign they see as destructive of human life. In the end, behind the hard actions of civil disobedience (soft in relation to the actions of government), there is a desire for a life in which all that will not be necessary. In these pages you will find Thoreau's essay "Life without Principle," published posthumously in 1863 in the *Atlantic Monthly* but expressing ideas developed through a number of lectures he gave between 1854 and 1860. Thoreau's final working title for the piece was "The Higher Law"; published today, it provides fresh insight into our very modern lives.

Here, he joins his criticism of government and society with his love of the natural world. How shall we live, he asks? "This world is a place of business." Money rules our lives but does not enrich them. "The ways by which you may get money almost without exception lead downward."

You read the newspapers, instead of walking in nature. The news we hear "is the stalest repetition." It is about large events, about governments, about nations. "Nations! What are nations? . . . Like insects, they swarm. The historian strives in vain to make them memorable." Thoreau would have appreciated Kurt Vonnegut, who places nations among those unnatural abstractions he calls "granfalloons" (*Cat's Cradle*), "a seeming team that was meaningless in terms of the ways God gets things done." What is "our boasted commerce," Thoreau asks, but "the activity of flies about a molasses-hogshead"? As for politics, it is "comparatively something so superficial and inhuman, that, practically, I have never fairly recognized that it concerns me at all."

Are Thoreau's ideas utopian? And are they therefore useless in a world of technological marvels, global commerce, and powerful nations? Or is it perhaps that Thoreau is asking that technology be tamed to serve our existential needs for peace and beauty, that commerce serve not greed, but human life, that nations be communities and not war machines? He is not against the "things" of modern life but wants to change the situation that Emerson described: "Things are in the saddle and ride mankind."

In the midst of the struggle for justice, however, Thoreau is convinced that right will prevail. Agitated as he is about the evil of slavery—"Who can be serene in a country where both the rulers and the ruled are without principle?"—he is brought back to himself when he scents a white water-lily and realizes that a season he "had waited for had arrived." The lily "suggests what kind of laws have prevailed longest and widest, and still prevail, and that the time may come when man's deeds will smell as sweet."

—Howard Zinn
December, 2003

The Higher Law

The Service

Qualities of the Recruit

> Spes sibi quisque. Virgil
> Each one his own hope.

THE brave man is the elder son of creation, who has stept boyantly into his inheritance, while the coward, who is the younger, waiteth patiently till he decease. He rides as wide of this earth's gravity as a star, and by yielding incessantly to all the impulses of the soul, is constantly drawn upward and becomes a fixed star. His bravery deals not so much in resolute action, as healthy and assured rest; its palmy state is a staying at home and compelling alliance in all directions. So stands his life to heaven, as some fair sunlit tree against the western horizon, and by sunrise is planted on some eastern hill, to glisten in the first rays of the dawn. The brave man braves nothing, nor knows he of his bravery. He is that sixth champion against Thebes, whom, when the proud devices of the rest have been recorded, the poet describes as "bearing a full orbed shield of solid brass,"

> "But there was no device upon its circle,
> For not to seem just but to be is his wish."

He does not present a gleaming edge to ward off harm, for that will oftenest attract the lightning, but rather is the all pervading ether, which the lightning does not strike but purify. So is the profanity of his companion as a flash across the face of his sky, which lights up and reveals its serene depths. Earth cannot shock the heavens, but its dull vapor and foul smoke make a bright cloud spot in the ether, and anon the sun, like a cunning artificer, will cut and paint it, and set it for a jewel in the breast of the sky.

His greatness is not measurable. His is not such a greatness as when we would erect a stupendous piece of art, and send far and near for materials, intending to lay the foundations deeper, and rear the structure higher, than ever, for hence results only a remarkable bulkiness without grandeur, lacking those true and simple proportions which are independent of size. He was not builded by that unwise generation, that would fain have reached the heavens by piling one brick upon another, but by a far wiser, that builded inward and not outward, having found out a shorter way, through the observance of a higher art. The pyramids some artisan may measure with his line; but if he give you the dimensions of the Parthenon in feet and inches, the figures will not embrace it like a cord, but dangle from its entablature like an elastic drapery.

His eye is the focus in which all the rays, from whatever side, are collected; for, itself being within and central, the entire circumference is revealed to it. Just as we scan the whole concave of the heavens at a glance, but can compass only one side of the pebble at our feet. So does his discretion give prevalence to his valor. "Discretion is the wise man's soul," saith the poet. His prudence may safely go many strides beyond the utmost rashness of the coward; for, while he observes strictly the golden mean, he seems to run through all extremes with impunity. Like the sun, which, to the poor worldling, now appears in the zenith, now in the horizon, and again is faintly reflected from the moon's disk, and has the credit of describing an entire great circle, crossing the equinoctial and solstitial colures, without detriment to his steadfastness or mediocrity. The golden mean, in ethics as in physics, is the center of the system, and that about which all revolve; and, though to a distant and plodding planet it be the uttermost extreme, yet one day, when that planet's year is complete, it will be found to be central. They who are alarmed lest Virtue should so far demean herself, as to be extremely good, have not yet wholly embraced her, but described only a slight arc of a few seconds about her, and from so small and ill defined a curvature, you can calculate no center whatever, but their mean is no better than meanness, nor their medium than mediocrity.

The coward wants resolution, which the brave man can do without. He recognizes no faith but a creed, thinking this straw, by which he is moored, does him good service, because his sheet anchor does not drag. "The house roof fights with the rain; he who is under shelter does not know it." In his religion, the ligature, which should be muscle and sinew, is rather like that thread which the accomplices of Cylon held in their hands, when they went abroad from the temple of Minerva, the other end being attached to the statue of the goddess. But frequently, as in their case, the thread breaks, being stretched, and he is left without an asylum.

The divinity in man is the true vestal fire of the temple, which is never permitted to go out, but burns as steadily, and with as pure a flame, on the obscure provincial altar, as in Numa's temple at Rome. In the meanest are all the materials of manhood, only they are not rightly disposed. We say justly that the weak person is flat, for like all flat substances, he does not stand in the direction of his strength, that is, on his edge, but affords a convenient surface to put upon. He slides all the way through life. Most

things are strong in one direction; a straw longitu-
dinally; a board in the direction of its edge; a knee
transversely to its grain; but the brave man is a
perfect sphere, which cannot fall on its flat side, and
is equally strong every way. The coward is wretchedly
spheroidal at best, too much educated or drawn out
on one side, and depressed on the other; or may be
likened to a hollow sphere, whose disposition of
matter is best when the greatest bulk is intended.

We shall not attain to be spherical by lying on one
or the other side for an eternity, but only by resigning
ourselves implicitly to the law of gravity in us, shall
we find our axis coincident with the celestial axis,
and by revolving incessantly through all circles, acquire a perfect sphericity. Mankind, like the earth,
revolve mainly from west to east, and so are flattened
at the poles. But does not philosophy give hint of a
movement commencing to be rotary at the poles too,
which in a millennium will have acquired increased
rapidity, and help restore an equilibrium? And when
at length every star in the nebulae and milky way,
has looked down with mild radiance for a season,
exerting its whole influence as the pole star, the demands of science will in some degree be satisfied.

The grand and majestic have always somewhat of
the undulatoriness of the sphere. It is the secret of
majesty in the rolling gait of the elephant, and of all
grace in action and in art. Always the line of beauty
is a curve. When with pomp a huge sphere is drawn
along the streets, by the efforts of a hundred men, I
seem to discover each striving to imitate its gait, and
keep step with it,—if possible to swell to its own
diameter. But onward it moves, and conquers the
multitude with its majesty. What shame then, that
our lives, which might so well be the source of plane-
tary motion, and sanction the order of the spheres,

should be full of abruptness and angulosity, so as not to roll nor move majestically.

The Romans "made Fortune sirname to Fortitude," for fortitude is that alchemy that turns all things to good fortune. The man of fortitude, whom the Latins called *fortis*, is no other than that lucky person whom *fors* favors, or *vir summae fortis*. If we will, every bark may "carry Caesar and Caesar's fortune." For an impenetrable shield, stand inside yourself; he was no artist, but an artisan, who first made shields of brass. For armor of proof, *meâ virtute me involvo*, I wrap myself in my virtue;

> "Tumble me down; and I will sit
> Upon my ruins, smiling yet."

If you let a single ray of light through the shutter, it will go on diffusing itself without limit till it enlighten the world, but the shadow that was never so wide at first, as rapidly contracts till it comes to naught. The shadow of the moon, when it passes nearest the sun, is lost in space ere it can reach our earth to eclipse it. Always the system shines with uninterrupted light, for as the sun is so much larger than any planet, no shadow can travel far into space. We may bask always in the light of the system, always may step back out of the shade. No man's shadow is as large as his body, if the rays make a right angle with the reflecting surface. Let our lives be passed under the equator, with the sun in the meridian.

There is no ill which may not be dissipated like the dark, if you let in a stronger light upon it. Overcome evil with good. Practise no such narrow economy as they, whose bravery amounts to no more light than a farthing candle, before which most objects cast a shadow wider than themselves.

Nature refuses to sympathize with our sorrow, she has not provided for, but by a thousand contrivances against it; she has bevelled the margins of the eyelids, that the tears may not overflow on the cheeks. It was a conceit of Plutarch, accounting for the preference given to signs observed on the left hand, that men may have thought "things terrestrial and mortal directly over against heavenly and divine things, and do conjecture that the things which to us are on the left hand, the gods send down from their right hand." If we are not blind, we shall see how a right hand is stretched over all, as well the unlucky as lucky, and that the ordering soul is only right handed, distributing with one palm all our fates.

What first suggested that necessity was grim, and made fate to be so fatal? The strongest is always the least violent. Necessity is my eastern cushion on which I recline. My eye revels in its prospect as in the summer haze. I ask no more but to be left alone with it. It is the bosom of time and the lap of eternity. To be necessary is to be needful, and necessity is only another name for inflexibility of good. How I welcome my grim fellow, and walk arm in arm with him. Let me too be such a Necessity as he. I love him, he is so flexile, and yields to me as the air to my body. I leap and dance in his midst, and play with his beard till he smiles. I greet thee my elder brother, who with thy touch ennoblest all things. Then is holiday when naught intervenes betwixt me and thee. Must it be so,—then is it good. The stars are thy interpreters to me.

Over Greece hangs the divine necessity ever a mellower heaven of itself, whose light gilds the Acropolis and a thousand fanes and groves.

What Music Shall We Have?

Each more melodious note I hear
Brings this reproach to me,
That I alone afford the ear,
Who would the music be.

THE brave man is the sole patron of music;
he recognizes it for his mother tongue; a more mellif-
luous and articulate language than words, in comparison with which, speech is recent and temporary.
It is his voice. His language must have the same
majestic movement and cadence, that philosophy as-
signs to the heavenly bodies. The steady flux of his
thought constitutes time in music. The universe falls
in and keeps pace with it, which before proceeded
singly and discordant. Hence are poetry and song.
When Bravery first grew afraid and went to war, it
took music along with it. The soul delighted still to
hear the echo of her own voice. Especially the soldier
insists on agreement and harmony always. To secure
these he falls out. Indeed, it is that friendship there
is in war that makes it chivalrous and heroic. It was
the dim sentiment of a noble friendship for the purest
soul the world has seen, that gave to Europe a crusad-
ing era. War is but the compelling of peace. If the
soldier marches to the sack of a town, he must be
preceded by drum and trumpet, which shall identify
his cause with the accordant universe. All things
thus echo back his own spirit, and thus the hostile
territory is preoccupied for him. He is no longer
insulated, but infinitely related and familiar. The roll
call musters for him all the forces of nature.

There is as much music in the world as virtue.
In a world of peace and love music would be the

universal language, and men greet each other in the fields in such accents, as a Beethoven now utters at rare intervals from a distance. All things obey music as they obey virtue. It is the herald of virtue. It is God's voice. In it are the centripetal and centrifugal forces. The universe needed only to hear a divine melody, that every star might fall into its proper place, and assume its true sphericity. It entails a surpassing affluence on the meanest thing; riding sublime over the heads of sages, and soothing the din of philosophy. When we listen to it we are so wise that we need not to know. All sounds, and more than all, silence, do fife and drum for us. The least creaking doth whet all our senses, and emit a tremulous light, like the aurora borealis, over things. As polishing expresses the vein in marble, and the grain in wood, so music brings out what of heroic lurks anywhere. It is either a sedative or a tonic to the soul. I read that "Plato thinks the gods never gave men music, the science of melody and harmony, for mere delectation or to tickle the ear; but that the discordant parts of the circulations, and beauteous fabric of the soul, and that of it that roves about the body, and many times for want of tune and air, breaks forth into many extravagances and excesses, might be sweetly recalled and artfully wound up to their former consent and agreement."

A sudden burst from a horn startles us, as if one had rashly provoked a wild beast. We admire his boldness, he dares wake the echoes which he cannot put to rest. The sound of a bugle in the stillness of the night, sends forth its voice to the farthest stars, and marshals them in new order and harmony. Instantly it finds a fit sounding board in the heavens. The notes flash out on the horizon like heat lightning, quickening the pulse of creation. The heavens say, Now is this my own earth.

To the sensitive soul the Universe has her own fixed measure and rhythm, which is its measure also and constitutes the regularity and health of its pulse. When the body marches to the measure of the soul then is true courage and invincible strength.

The coward would reduce this thrilling sphere music to a universal wail,—this melodious chant to a nasal cant. He thinks to conciliate all hostile influences by compelling his neighborhood into a partial concord with himself, but his music is no better than a jingle, which is akin to a jar,—jars regularly recurring. He blows a feeble blast of slender melody, because nature can have no more sympathy with such a soul, than it has of cheerful melody in itself. Hence hears he no accordant note in the universe, and is a coward, or consciously outcast and deserted man. But the brave man, without drum or trumpet, compels concord everywhere by the universality and tunefulness of his soul.

Let not the faithful sorrow that he has no ear for the more fickle and subtle harmonies of creation, if he be awake to the slower measure of virtue and truth. If his pulse does not beat in unison with the musician's quips and turns, it accords with the pulse beat of the ages.

A man's life should be a stately march to an unheard music, and when to his fellows it seems irregular and inharmonious, he will be stepping to a livelier measure, which only his nicer ear can detect. There will be no halt ever, but at most a marching on his post, or such a pause as is richer than any sound—when the deepened melody is no longer heard, but implicitly consented to with the whole life and being. He will take a false step never, even in the most arduous circumstances, for then the music will not fail to swell into corresponding volume and distinctness and rule the movement it accompanies.

Not How Many But Where the Enemy Are

> "What's brave, what's noble,
> Let's do it after the high Roman fashion."
> Shakspeare

WHEN my eye falls on the stupendous masses of the clouds, tossed into such irregular greatness across the cope of my sky, I feel that their grandeur is thrown away on the meanness of my employment. In vain the sun through morning and noon rolls defiance to man, and, as he sinks behind his cloudy fortress in the west, challenges him to equal greatness in his career; but from his humbleness he looks up to the domes, and minarets, and gilded battlements of the eternal city, and is content to be a suburban dweller outside the walls. We look in vain over earth for a Roman greatness, to take up the gauntlet which the heavens throw down. Idomeneus would not have demurred at the freshness of the last morning that rose to us, as unfit occasion to display his valor in; and of some such evening as this, methinks, that Greek fleet came to anchor in the bay of Aulis. Would that it were to us the eve of a more than ten years' war, a tithe of whose exploits, and Achillean withdrawals, and godly interferences, would stock a library of Iliads. Better that we have some of that testy spirit of knight errantry, and if we are so blind as to think the world is not rich enough nowadays to afford a real foe to combat, with our trusty swords and double handed maces, hew and mangle some unreal phantom of the brain. In the pale and shivering fogs of the morning, gathering them up betimes, and withdrawing sluggishly to their daylight haunts, I see Falsehood sneaking from the full blaze of truth, and with good relish could do execution on their rearward ranks with the first brand that came to hand. We too are such puny creatures as to be put to flight by the sun, and suffer our ardor to grow cool in proportion as his increases; our own short lived chivalry sounds a retreat with the fumes and vapors of the night, and we turn to meet mankind with its meek face preaching peace, and such nonresistance as the chaff that rides before the whirlwind. Let not our Peace be proclaimed by the rust on our swords, or our inability to draw them from their scabbards, but let her at least have so much work on her hands, as to keep those swords bright and sharp. The very dogs that bay the moon from farmyards o' these nights, do evince more heroism than is tamely barked forth in all the civil exhortations and war sermons of the age. And that day and night, which should be set down indelibly in men's hearts, must be learned from the pages of an almanack. One cannot wonder at the owlish habits of the race, which does not distinguish when its day ends and night begins, for as night is the season of rest, it would be hard to say when its toil ended and its rest began. Not to it

—returns
Day, or the sweet approach of even or morn,
Or sight of vernal bloom, or summer's rose,
Or flocks, or herds, or human face divine;
But cloud instead, and ever-during dark
Surrounds—

And so the time lapses without epoch or era, and we know some half score of mornings and evenings by tradition only. Almost the night is grieved and leaves her tears on the forelock of day, that men will not rush to her embrace, and fulfil, at length, the pledge so forwardly given in the youth of time. Men are a circumstance to themselves, instead of causing the universe to stand around the mute witness of their manhood, and the stars to forget their sphere music and chant an elegiac strain, that heroism should have departed out of their ranks and gone over to humanity.

It is not enough that our life is an easy one; we must live on the stretch, retiring to our rest like soldiers on the eve of a battle, looking forward with ardor to the strenuous sortie of the morrow. "Sit not down in the popular seats and common level of virtues, but endeavor to make them heroical. Offer not only peace offerings but holocausts unto God." To the brave soldier the rust and leisure of peace are harder than the fatigues of war. As our bodies court physical encounters, and languish in the mild and even climate of the tropics, so our souls thrive best on unrest and discontent. The soul is a sterner master than any King Frederick, for a true bravery would subject our bodies to rougher usage than even a grenadier could withstand. We too are dwellers within the purlieus of the camp. When the sun breaks through the morning mist, I seem to hear the din of war louder than when his chariot thundered on the plains of Troy. The thin fields of vapor spread like gauze over the woods, form extended lawns whereon high tournament is held

before each van
Prick forth the aery knights, and couch their spears,
Till thickest legions close.

It behoves us to make life a steady progression, and not be defeated by its opportunities. The stream which first fell a drop from heaven, should be filtered by events till it burst out into springs of greater purity, and extract a diviner flavor from the accidents through which it passes. Shall man wear out sooner than the sun, and not rather dawn as freshly, and with such native dignity stalk down the hills of the east into the bustling vale of life, with as lofty and serene a countenance to roll onward through midday, to a yet fairer and more promising setting? In the crimson colors of the west I discern the budding hues of dawn. To my western brother it is rising pure and bright as it did to me, but only the evening exhibits in the still rear of day, the beauty which through morning and noon escaped me. Is not that which we call the gross atmosphere of evening the accumulated deed of the day, which absorbs the rays of beauty, and shows more richly than the naked promise of the dawn? Let us look to it, that by earnest toil in the heat of the noon, we get ready a rich western blaze against the evening.

Nor need we fear that the time will hang heavy when our toil is done, for our task is not such a piece of day labor, that a man must be thinking what he shall do next for a livelihood, but such, that as it began in endeavor, so will it end only when no more in heaven or on earth remains to be endeavored. Effort is the prerogative of virtue. Let not death be the sole task of life, the moment when we are rescued from death to life. And set to work,—if indeed that can be called a task which all things do but alleviate. Nor will we suffer our hands to lose one jot of their handiness by looking behind to a mean recompense, knowing that our endeavor cannot be thwarted, nor we be cheated of our earnings unless by not earning them.

It concerns us rather to be somewhat here present than to leave something behind us; for, if that were to be considered, it is never the deed men praise, but some marble or canvass which are only a staging to the real work. The hugest and most effective deed may have no sensible result at all on earth, but may paint itself in the heavens with new stars and constellations. When in rare moments our whole being strives with one consent, which we name a yearning, we may not hope that our work will stand in any artist's gallery on earth. The bravest deed, which for the most part is left quite out of history, which alone wants the staleness of a deed done, and the uncertainty of a deed doing, is the life of a great man. To perform exploits is to be temporarily bold, as becomes a courage that ebbs and flows, the soul quite vanquished by its own deed subsiding into indifference and cowardice, but the exploit of a brave life consists in its momentary completeness.

Every stroke of the chisel must enter our own flesh and bone, he is a mere idolater and apprentice to art who suffers it to grate dully on marble; for the true art is not merely a sublime consolation, and holiday labor, which the gods have given to sickly mortals, but such a masterpiece, as you may imagine a dweller on the table lands of central Asia might produce, with threescore and ten years for canvass, and the faculties of a man for tools,—a human life,—wherein you might hope to discover more than the freshness of Guido's Aurora, or the mild light of Titian's landscapes;—no bald imitation nor even rival of nature, but rather the restored original of which she is the reflection. For such a masterpiece as this, whole galleries of Greece and Italy are a mere mixing of colors and preparatory quarrying of marble.

Of such sort, then, be our crusade, which, while it inclines chiefly to the hearty good will and activity of war, rather than the insincerity and sloth of peace, will set an example to both of calmness and energy;— as unconcerned for victory as careless of defeat, not seeking to lengthen our term of service, nor to cut it short by a reprieve, but earnestly applying ourselves to the campaign before us. Nor let our warfare be a boorish and uncourteous one, but a higher courtesy attend its higher chivalry, though not to the slackening of its tougher duties and severer discipline; that so our camp may be a palaestra, wherein the dormant energies and affections of men may tug and wrestle, not to their discomfiture, but to their mutual exercise and development.

What were Godfrey and Gonzalo unless we breathed a life into them, and enacted their exploits as a prelude to our own? The past is the canvass on which our idea is painted,—the dim prospectus of our future field. We are dreaming of what we are to do. Methinks I hear the clarion sound, and clang of corselet and buckler, from many a silent hamlet of the soul. The signal gun has long since sounded and we are not yet on our posts. Let us make such haste as the morning, and such delay as the evening.

Paradise (To Be) Regained*

WE learn that Mr. Etzler is a native of Germany, and originally published his book in Pennsylvania, ten or twelve years ago; and now a second English edition, from the original American one, is demanded by his readers across the water, owing, we suppose, to the recent spread of Fourier's doctrines. It is one of the signs of the times. We confess that we have risen from reading this book with enlarged ideas, and grander conceptions of our duties in this world. It did expand us a little. It is worth attending to, if only that it entertains large questions. Consider what Mr. Etzler proposes:

"Fellow Men! I promise to show the means of creating a paradise within ten years, where everything desirable for human life may be had by every man in superabundance, without labor, and without pay; where the whole face of nature shall be changed into the most beautiful forms, and man may live in the most magnificent palaces, in all imaginable refinements of luxury, and in the most delightful gardens; where he may accomplish, without labor, in one year, more than hitherto could be done in thousands of years; may level mountains, sink valleys, create lakes, drain lakes and swamps, and intersect the land everywhere with beautiful canals, and roads for transporting heavy loads of many thousand tons, and for travelling one thousand miles in twenty-four hours; may cover the ocean with floating islands movable in any desired direction with immense power and celerity, in perfect security, and with all comforts and luxuries, bearing gardens and palaces, with thousands of families, and provided with rivulets of sweet water; may explore the interior of the globe, and travel from pole to pole in a fortnight; provide himself with means, unheard of yet,

* The Paradise within the Reach of all Men, without Labor, by Powers of Nature and Machinery. An Address to all intelligent Men. In two parts. By J. A. Etzler. Part First. Second English Edition. pp. 55. London, 1842.

for increasing his knowledge of the world, and so his intelligence; lead a life of continual happiness, of enjoyments yet unknown; free himself from almost all the evils that afflict mankind, except death, and even put death far beyond the common period of human life, and finally render it less afflicting. Mankind may thus live in and enjoy a new world, far superior to the present, and raise themselves far higher in the scale of being."

It would seem from this and various indications beside, that there is a transcendentalism in mechanics as well as in ethics. While the whole field of the one reformer lies beyond the boundaries of space, the other is pushing his schemes for the elevation of the race to its utmost limits. While one scours the heavens, the other sweeps the earth. One says he will reform himself, and then nature and circumstances will be right. Let us not obstruct ourselves, for that is the greatest friction. It is of little importance though a cloud obstruct the view of the astronomer compared with his own blindness. The other will reform nature and circumstances, and then man will be right. Talk no more vaguely, says he, of reforming the world—I will reform the globe itself. What matters it whether I remove this humor out of my flesh, or the pestilent humor from the fleshy part of the globe? Nay, is not the latter the more generous course? At present the globe goes with a shattered constitution in its orbit. Has it not asthma, and ague, and fever, and dropsy, and flatulence, and pleurisy, and is it not afflicted with vermin? Has it not its healthful laws counteracted, and its vital energy which will yet redeem it? No doubt the simple powers of nature properly directed by man would make it healthy and paradise; as the laws of man's own constitution but wait to be obeyed, to restore him to health and happiness. Our panaceas cure but few ails, our general hospitals are private and exclusive.

We must set up another Hygeian than is now worshipped. Do not the quacks even direct small doses for children, larger for adults, and larger still for oxen and horses? Let us remember that we are to prescribe for the globe itself.

This fair homestead has fallen to us, and how little have we done to improve it, how little have we cleared and hedged and ditched! We are too inclined to go hence to a "better land," without lifting a finger, as our farmers are moving to the Ohio soil; but would it not be more heroic and faithful to till and redeem this New-England soil of the world? The still youthful energies of the globe have only to be directed in their proper channel. Every gazette brings accounts of the untutored freaks of the wind—shipwrecks and hurricanes which the mariner and planter accept as special or general providences; but they touch our consciences, they remind us of our sins. Another deluge would disgrace mankind. We confess we never had much respect for that antediluvian race. A thorough-bred business man cannot enter heartily upon the business of life without first looking into his accounts. How many things are now at loose ends. Who knows which way the wind will blow to-morrow? Let us not succumb to nature. We will marshal the clouds and restrain the tempests; we will bottle up pestilent exhalations, we will probe for earthquakes, grub them up; and give vent to the dangerous gases; we will disembowel the volcano, and extract its poison, take its seed out. We will wash water, and warm fire, and cool ice, and underprop the earth. We will teach birds to fly, and fishes to swim, and ruminants to chew the cud. It is time we had looked into these things.

And it becomes the moralist, too, to inquire what man might do to improve and beautify the system;

what to make the stars shine more brightly, the sun more cheery and joyous, the moon more placid and content. Could he not heighten the tints of flowers and the melody of birds? Does he perform his duty to the inferior races? Should he not be a god to them? What is the part of magnanimity to the whale and the beaver? Should we not fear to exchange places with them for a day, lest by their behavior they should shame us? Might we not treat with magnanimity the shark and the tiger, not descend to meet them on their own level, with spears of sharks' teeth and bucklers of tiger's skin? We slander the hyena; man is the fiercest and cruelest animal. Ah! he is of little faith; even the erring comets and meteors would thank him, and return his kindness in their kind.

How meanly and grossly do we deal with nature! Could we not have a less gross labor? What else do these fine inventions suggest,—magnetism, the daguerreotype, electricity? Can we not do more than cut and trim the forest,—can we not assist in its interior economy, in the circulation of the sap? Now we work superficially and violently. We do not suspect how much might be done to improve our relation with animated nature; what kindness and refined courtesy there might be.

There are certain pursuits which, if not wholly poetic and true, do at least suggest a nobler and finer relation to nature than we know. The keeping of bees, for instance, is a very slight interference. It is like directing the sunbeams. All nations, from the remotest antiquity, have thus fingered nature. There are Hymettus and Hybla, and how many bee-renowned spots beside? There is nothing gross in the idea of these little herds,—their hum like the faintest low of kine in the meads. A pleasant reviewer has lately reminded us that in some places they are led out to pasture where the flowers are most abundant. "Columella tells us," says he, "that the inhabitants of Arabia sent their hives into Attica to benefit by the later-blowing flowers." Annually are the hives, in immense pyramids, carried up the Nile in boats, and suffered to float slowly down the stream by night, resting by day, as the flowers put forth along the banks; and they determine the richness of any locality, and so the profitableness of delay, by the sinking of the boat in the water. We are told, by the same reviewer, of a man in Germany, whose bees yielded more honey than those of his neighbors, with no apparent advantage; but at length he informed them that he had turned his hives one degree more to the east, and so his bees, having two hours the start in the morning, got the first sip of honey. True, there is treachery and selfishness behind all this; but these things suggest to the poetic mind what might be done.

Many examples there are of a grosser interference, yet not without their apology. We saw last summer, on the side of a mountain, a dog employed to churn for a farmer's family, travelling upon a horizontal wheel, and though he had sore eyes, an alarming cough, and withal a demure aspect, yet their bread did get buttered for all that. Undoubtedly, in the most brilliant successes, the first rank is always sacrificed. Much useless travelling of horses, *in extenso*, has of late years been improved for man's behoof, only two forces being taken advantage of,— the gravity of the horse, which is the centripetal, and his centrifugal inclination to go a-head. Only these two elements in the calculation. And is not the creature's whole economy better economized thus? Are not all finite beings better pleased with motions relative than absolute? And what is the great globe itself but such a wheel,—a larger tread-mill,—so that our horse's freest steps over prairies are oftentimes balked and rendered of no avail by the earth's motion on its axis? But here he is the central agent and motive power; and, for variety of scenery, being provided with a window in front, do not the ever-varying activity and fluctuating energy of the creature himself work the effect of the most varied scenery on a country road? It must be confessed that horses at present work too exclusively for men, rarely men for horses; and the brute degenerates in man's society.

It will be seen that we contemplate a time when man's will shall be law to the physical world, and he shall no longer be deterred by such abstractions as time and space, height and depth, weight and hardness, but shall indeed be the lord of creation. "Well," says the faithless reader, " 'life is short, but art is long;' where is the power that will effect all these changes?" This it is the very object of Mr. Etzler's volume to show. At present, he would merely remind us that there are innumerable and immeasurable powers already existing in nature, unimproved on a large scale, or for generous and universal ends, amply sufficient for these purposes. He would only indicate their existence, as a surveyor makes known the existence of a water-power on any stream; but for their application he refers us to a sequel to this book, called the "Mechanical System." A few of the most obvious and familiar of these powers are, the Wind, the Tide, the Waves, the Sunshine. Let us consider their value.

First, there is the power of the Wind, constantly exerted over the globe. It appears from observation of a sailing-vessel, and from scientific tables, that the

average power of the wind is equal to that of one
horse for every one hundred square feet. "We know,"
says our author—

"that ships of the first class carry sails two hundred feet
high; we may, therefore, equally, on land, oppose to the
wind surfaces of the same height. Imagine a line of such
surfaces one mile, or about 5,000 feet, long; they would
then contain 1,000,000 square feet. Let these surfaces
intersect the direction of the wind at right angles, by
some contrivance, and receive, consequently, its full
power at all times. Its average power being equal to one
horse for every 100 square feet, the total power would be
equal to 1,000,000 divided by 100, or 10,000 horses' power.
Allowing the power of one horse to equal that of ten men,
the power of 10,000 horses is equal to 100,000 men. But
as men cannot work uninterruptedly, but want about half
the time for sleep and repose, the same power would be
equal to 200,000 men. . . . We are not limited to the
height of 200 feet; we might extend, if required, the application of this power to the height of the clouds, by
means of kites."

But we will have one such fence for every square
mile of the globe's surface, for, as the wind usually
strikes the earth at an angle of more than two degrees, which is evident from observing its effect on
the high sea, it admits of even a closer approach. As
the surface of the globe contains about 200,000,000
square miles, the whole power of the wind on these
surfaces would equal 40,000,000,000,000 men's power, and "would perform 80,000 times as much work
as all the men on earth could effect with their
nerves."

If it should be objected that this computation in-
cludes the surface of the ocean and uninhabitable
regions of the earth, where this power could not be
applied for our purposes, Mr. Etzler is quick with his
reply—"But, you will recollect," says he, "that I have
promised to show the means for rendering the ocean

as inhabitable as the most fruitful dry land; and I do not exclude even the polar regions."

The reader will observe that our author uses the fence only as a convenient formula for expressing the power of the wind, and does not consider it a necessary method of its application. We do not attach much value to this statement of the comparative power of the wind and horse, for no common ground is mentioned on which they can be compared. Undoubtedly, each is incomparably excellent in its way, and every general comparison made for such practical purposes as are contemplated, which gives a preference to the one, must be made with some unfairness to the other. The scientific tables are, for the most part, true only in a tabular sense. We suspect that a loaded wagon, with a light sail, ten feet square, would not have been blown so far by the end of the year, under equal circumstances, as a common racer or dray horse would have drawn it. And how many crazy structures on our globe's surface, of the same dimensions, would wait for dry-rot if the traces of one horse were hitched to them, even to their windward side? Plainly, this is not the principle of comparison. But even the steady and constant force of the horse may be rated as equal to his weight at least. Yet we should prefer to let the zephyrs and gales bear, with all their weight, upon our fences, than that Dobbin, with feet braced, should lean ominously against them for a season.

Nevertheless, here is an almost incalculable power at our disposal, yet how trifling the use we make of it. It only serves to turn a few mills, blow a few vessels across the ocean, and a few trivial ends besides. What a poor compliment do we pay to our indefatigable and energetic servant!

"If you ask, perhaps, why this power is not used, if the statement be true, I have to ask in return, why is the power of steam so lately come to application? so many millions of men boiled water every day for many thousand years; they must have frequently seen that boiling water, in tightly closed pots or kettles, would lift the cover or burst the vessel with great violence. The power of steam was, therefore, as commonly known down to the least kitchen or wash-woman, as the power of wind; but close observation and reflection were bestowed neither on the one nor the other."

Men having discovered the power of falling water, which after all is comparatively slight, how eagerly do they seek out and improve these *privileges*? Let a difference of but a few feet in level be discovered on some stream near a populous town, some slight occasion for gravity to act, and the whole economy of the neighborhood is changed at once. Men do indeed speculate about and with this power as if it were the only privilege. But meanwhile this aerial stream is falling from far greater heights with more constant flow, never shrunk by drought, offering mill-sites wherever the wind blows; a Niagara in the air, with no Canada side;—only the application is hard.

There are the powers too of the Tide and Waves, constantly ebbing and flowing, lapsing and relapsing, but they serve man in but few ways. They turn a few tide mills, and perform a few other insignificant and accidental services only. We all perceive the effect of the tide; how imperceptibly it creeps up into our harbors and rivers, and raises the heaviest navies as easily as the lightest ship. Everything that floats must yield to it. But man, slow to take nature's constant hint of assistance, makes slight and irregular use of this power, in careening ships and getting them afloat when aground.

The following is Mr. Etzler's calculation on this head: To form a conception of the power which the tide affords, let us imagine a surface of 100 miles square, or 10,000 square miles, where the tide rises and sinks, on an average, 10 feet; how many men would it require to empty a basin of 10,000 square miles area, and 10 feet deep, filled with sea-water, in 6¼ hours and fill it again in the same time? As one man can raise 8 cubic feet of sea-water per minute, and in 6¼ hours 3,000, it would take 1,200,000,000 men, or as they could work only half the time, 2,400,-000,000, to raise 3,000,000,000,000 cubic feet, or the whole quantity required in the given time.

This power may be applied in various ways. A large body, of the heaviest materials that will float, may first be raised by it, and being attached to the end of a balance reaching from the land, or from a stationary support, fastened to the bottom, when the tide falls, the whole weight will be brought to bear upon the end of the balance. Also when the tide rises it may be made to exert a nearly equal force in the opposite direction. It can be employed whenever a *point d'appui* can be obtained.

"However, the application of the tide being by establishments fixed on the ground, it is natural to begin with them near the shores in shallow water, and upon sands, which may be extended gradually further into the sea. The shores of the continent, islands, and sands, being generally surrounded by shallow water, not exceeding from 50 to 100 fathoms in depth, for 20, 50, or 100 miles and upward. The coasts of North America, with their extensive sand-banks, islands, and rocks, may easily afford, for this purpose, a ground about 3,000 miles long, and, on an average, 100 miles broad, or 300,000 square miles, which, with a power of 240,000 men per square mile, as stated, at 10 feet tide, will be equal to 72,000 millions of men, or for every mile of coast, a power of 24,000,000 men."

"Rafts, of any extent, fastened on the ground of the sea, along the shore, and stretching far into the sea, may be covered with fertile soil, bearing vegetables and trees, of every description, the finest gardens, equal to those the firm land may admit of, and buildings and machineries, which may operate, not only on the sea, where they are, but which also, by means of mechanical connections, may extend their operations for many miles into the continent. (Etzler's Mechanical System, page 24.) Thus this power may cultivate the artificial soil for many miles upon the surface of the sea, near the shores, and, for several miles, the dry land, along the shore, in the most superior manner imaginable; it may build cities along the shore, consisting of the most magnificent palaces, every one surrounded by gardens and the most delightful sceneries; it may level the hills and unevennesses, or raise eminences for enjoying open prospect into the country and upon the sea; it may cover the barren shore with fertile soil, and beautify the same in various ways; it may clear the sea of shallows, and make easy the approach to the land, not merely of vessels, but of large floating islands, which may come from, and go to distant parts of the world, islands that have every commodity and security for their inhabitants which the firm land affords."

"Thus may a power, derived from the gravity of the moon and the ocean, hitherto but the objects of idle curiosity to the studious man, be made eminently subservient for creating the most delightful abodes along the coasts, where men may enjoy at the same time all the advantages of sea and dry land; the coasts may hereafter be continuous paradisiacal skirts between land and sea, everywhere crowded with the densest population. The shores and the sea along them will be no more as raw nature presents them now, but everywhere of easy and charming access, not even molested by the roar of waves, shaped as it may suit the purposes of their inhabitants; the sea will be cleared of every obstruction to free passage every-where, and its productions in fishes, etc., will be gathered in large, appropriate receptacles, to present them to the inhabitants of the shores and of the sea."

Verily, the land would wear a busy aspect at the spring and neap tide, and these island ships—these *terræ infirmæ*—which realise the fables of antiquity, affect our imagination. We have often thought that the fittest locality for a human dwelling was on the edge of the land, that there the constant lesson and impression of the sea might sink deep into the life and character of the landsman, and perhaps impart a marine tint to his imagination. It is a noble word, that *mariner*—one who is conversant with the sea. There should be more of what it signifies in each of us. It is a worthy country to belong to—we look to see him not disgrace it. Perhaps we should be equally mariners and terreners, and even our Green Mountains need some of that sea-green to be mixed with them.

The computation of the power of the waves is less satisfactory. While only the average power of the wind, and the average height of the tide, were taken before now, the extreme height of the waves is used, for they are made to rise ten feet above the level of the sea, to which, adding ten more for depression, we have twenty feet, or the extreme height of a wave. Indeed, the power of the waves, which is produced by the wind blowing obliquely and at disadvantage upon the water, is made to be, not only three thousand times greater than that of the tide, but one hundred times greater than that of the wind itself, meeting its object at right angles. Moreover, this power is measured by the area of the vessel, and not by its length mainly, and it seems to be forgotten that the motion of the waves is chiefly undulatory, and exerts a power only within the limits of a vibration, else the very continents, with their extensive coasts, would soon be set adrift.

Finally, there is the power to be derived from

sunshine, by the principle on which Archimedes
contrived his burning mirrors, a multiplication of
mirrors reflecting the rays of the sun upon the same
spot, till the requisite degree of heat is obtained. The
principal application of this power will be to the
boiling of water and production of steam.

"How to create rivulets of sweet and wholesome water,
on floating islands, in the midst of the ocean, will be no
riddle now. Sea-water changed into steam, will distil into
sweet water, leaving the salt on the bottom. Thus the
steam engines on floating islands, for their propulsion
and other mechanical purposes, will serve, at the same
time, for the distillery of sweet water, which, collected in
basins, may be led through channels over the island,
while, where required, it may be refrigerated by artificial
means, and changed into cool water, surpassing, in salu-
brity, the best spring water, because nature hardly ever
distils water so purely, and without admixture of less
wholesome matter."

So much for these few and more obvious powers,
already used to a trifling extent. But there are innumerable others in nature, not described nor discovered. These, however, will do for the present. This
would be to make the sun and the moon equally
our satellites. For, as the moon is the cause of the
tides, and the sun the cause of the wind, which, in
turn, is the cause of the waves, all the work of this
planet would be performed by these far influences.

"But as these powers are very irregular and subject to
interruptions; the next object is to show how they may be
converted into powers that operate continually and uni-
formly for ever, until the machinery be worn out, or, in
other words, into perpetual motions." . . . "Hitherto the
power of the wind has been applied immediately upon
the machinery for use, and we have had to wait the
chances of the wind's blowing; while the operation was
stopped as soon as the wind ceased to blow. But the
manner, which I shall state hereafter, of applying this

power, is to make it operate only for collecting or storing up power, and then to take out of this store, at any time, as much as may be wanted for final operation upon the machines. The power stored up is to react as required, and may do so long after the original power of the wind has ceased. And though the wind should cease for intervals of many months, we may have by the same power a uniform perpetual motion in a very simple way."

"The weight of a clock being wound up gives us an image of reaction. The sinking of this weight is the reaction of winding it up. It is not necessary to wait till it has run down before we wind up the weight, but it may be wound up at any time, partly or totally; and if done always before the weight reaches the bottom, the clock will be going perpetually. In a similar, though not in the same way, we may cause a reaction on a larger scale. We may raise, for instance, water by the immediate application of wind or steam to a pond upon some eminence, out of which, through an outlet, it may fall upon some wheel or other contrivance for setting machinery a going. Thus we may store up water in some eminent pond, and take out of this store, at any time, as much water through the outlet as we want to employ, by which means the original power may react for many days after it has ceased." . . . "Such reservoirs of moderate elevation or size need not be made artificially, but will be found made by nature very frequently, requiring but little aid for their completion. They require no regularity of form. Any valley with lower grounds in its vicinity, would answer the purpose. Small crevices may be filled up. Such places may be eligible for the beginning of enterprises of this kind."

The greater the height, of course the less water required. But suppose a level and dry country; then hill and valley, and "eminent pond," are to be constructed by main force; or if the springs are unusually low, then dirt and stones may be used, and the disadvantage arising from friction will be counterbalanced by their greater gravity. Nor shall a single rood of dry land be sunk in such artificial ponds as may be wasted, but their surfaces "may be covered with rafts decked with fertile earth, and all kinds of vegetables which may grow there as well as anywhere else."

And finally, by the use of thick envelopes retaining the heat, and other contrivances, "the power of steam caused by sunshine may react at will, and thus be rendered perpetual, no matter how often or how long the sunshine may be interrupted. (Etzler's Mechanical System)."

Here is power enough, one would think, to accomplish somewhat. These are the powers below. Oh ye millwrights, ye engineers, ye operatives and speculators of every class, never again complain of a want of power; it is the grossest form of infidelity. The question is not how we shall execute, but what. Let us not use in a niggardly manner what is thus generously offered.

Consider what revolutions are to be effected in agriculture. First, in the new country, a machine is to move along taking out trees and stones to any required depth, and piling them up in convenient heaps; then the same machine, "with a little alteration," is to plane the ground perfectly, till there shall be no hills nor valleys, making the requisite canals, ditches and roads, as it goes along. The same machine, "with some other little alterations," is then to sift the ground thoroughly, supply fertile soil from other places if wanted, and plant it; and finally, the same machine "with a little addition," is to reap and gather in the crop, thresh and grind it, or press it to oil, or prepare it any way for final use. For the description of these machines we are referred to "Etzler's Mechanical System, pages 11 to 27." We should be pleased to see that "Mechanical System," though we have not been able to ascertain whether it has been published, or only exists as yet in the design of the author. We have great faith in it. But we cannot stop for applications now.

"Any wilderness, even the most hideous and sterile, may be converted into the most fertile and delightful gardens. The most dismal swamps may be cleared of all their spontaneous growth, filled up and levelled, and intersected by canals, ditches and aqueducts, for draining them entirely. The soil, if required, may be meliorated, by covering or mixing it with rich soil taken from distant places, and the same be mouldered to fine dust, levelled, sifted from all roots, weeds and stones, and sowed and planted in the most beautiful order and symmetry, with fruit trees and vegetables of every kind that may stand the climate."

New facilities for transportation and locomotion are to be adopted:

"Large and commodious vehicles, for carrying many thousand tons, running over peculiarly adapted level roads, at the rate of forty miles per hour, or one thousand miles per day, may transport men and things, small houses, and whatever may serve for comfort and ease, by land. Floating islands, constructed of logs, or of wooden-stuff prepared in a similar manner, as is to be done with stone, and of live trees, which may be reared so as to interlace one another, and strengthen the whole, may be covered with gardens and palaces, and propelled by powerful engines, so as to run at an equal rate through seas and oceans. Thus, man may move, with the celerity of a bird's flight, in terrestrial paradises, from one climate to another, and see the world in all its variety, exchanging, with distant nations, the surplus of productions. The journey from one pole to another may be performed in a fortnight; the visit to a transmarine country in a week or two; or a journey round the world in one or two months by land and water. And why pass a dreary winter every year while there is yet room enough on the globe where nature is blessed with a perpetual summer, and with a far greater variety and luxuriance of vegetation? More than one-half the surface of the globe has no winter. Men will have it in their power to remove and pre-

vent all bad influences of climate, and to enjoy, perpetually, only that temperature which suits their constitution
and feeling best."

Who knows but by accumulating the power until
the end of the present century, using meanwhile only
the smallest allowance, reserving all that blows, all
that shines, all that ebbs and flows, all that dashes,
we may have got such a reserved accumulated power
as to run the earth off its track into a new orbit, some
summer, and so change the tedious vicissitude of the
seasons? Or, perchance, coming generations will not
abide the dissolution of the globe, but, availing themselves of future inventions in aerial locomotion, and
the navigation of space, the entire race may migrate
from the earth, to settle some vacant and more western planet, it may be still healthy, perchance un-
earthy, not composed of dirt and stones, whose pri-
mary strata only are strewn, and where no weeds are
sown. It took but little art, a simple application of
natural laws, a canoe, a paddle, and a sail of matting,
to people the isles of the Pacific, and a little more
will people the shining isles of space. Do we not see
in the firmament the lights carried along the shore
by night, as Columbus did? Let us not despair nor
mutiny.

"The dwellings also ought to be very different from
what is known, if the full benefit of our means is to be
enjoyed. They are to be of a structure for which we have
no name yet. They are to be neither palaces, nor temples,
nor cities, but a combination of all, superior to whatever
is known. Earth may be baked into bricks, or even vitrified
stone by heat,—we may bake large masses of any size and
form into stone and vitrified substance of the greatest
durability, lasting even thousands of years, out of clayey
earth, or of stones ground to dust, by the application of
burning mirrors. This is to be done in the open air, without other preparation than gathering the substance, grinding and mixing it with water and cement, moulding or

casting it, and bringing the focus of the burning mirrors of proper size upon the same. The character of the architecture is to be quite different from what it ever has been hitherto; large solid masses are to be baked or cast in one piece, ready shaped in any form that may be desired. The building may, therefore, consist of columns two hundred feet high and upwards, of proportionate thickness, and of one entire piece of vitrified substance; huge pieces are to be moulded so as to join and hook on to each other firmly, by proper joints and folds, and not to yield in any way without breaking."

"Foundries, of any description, are to be heated by burning mirrors, and will require no labor, except the making of the first moulds and the superintendence for gathering the metal and taking the finished articles away."

Alas, in the present state of science, we must take the finished articles away; but think not that man will always be a victim of circumstances.

The countryman who visited the city and found the streets cluttered with bricks and lumber, reported that it was not yet finished, and one who considers the endless repairs and reforming of our houses, might well wonder when they will be done. But why may not the dwellings of men on this earth be built once for all of some durable material, some Roman or Etruscan masonry which will stand, so that time shall only adorn and beautify them? Why may we not finish the outward world for posterity, and leave them leisure to attend to the inner? Surely, all the gross necessities and economies might be cared for in a few years. All might be built and baked and stored up, during this, the term-time of the world, against the vacant eternity, and the globe go provisioned and furnished like our public vessels, for its voyage through space, as through some Pacific ocean, while we would "tie up the rudder and sleep before the wind," as those who sail from Lima to Manilla.

But, to go back a few years in imagination, think

not that life in these crystal palaces is to bear any analogy to life in our present humble cottages. Far from it. Clothed, once for all, in some "flexible stuff," more durable than George Fox's suit of leather, composed of "fibres of vegetables," "glutinated" together by some "cohesive substances," and made into sheets, like paper, of any size or form, man will put far from him corroding care and the whole host of ills.

"The twenty-five halls in the inside of the square are to be each two hundred feet square and high; the forty corridors, each one hundred feet long and twenty wide; the eighty galleries, each from 1,000 to 1,250 feet long; about 7,000 private rooms, the whole surrounded and intersected by the grandest and most splendid colonnades imaginable; floors, ceilings, columns with their various beautiful and fanciful intervals, all shining, and reflecting to infinity all objects and persons, with splendid lustre of all beautiful colors, and fanciful shapes and pictures. All galleries, outside and within the halls, are to be provided with many thousand commodious and most elegant vehicles, in which persons may move up and down, like birds, in perfect security, and without exertion. Any member may procure himself all the common articles of his daily wants, by a short turn of some crank, without leaving his apartment; he may, at any time, bathe himself in cold or warm water, or in steam, or in some artificially prepared liquor for invigorating health. He may, at any time, give to the air in his apartment that temperature that suits his feeling best. He may cause, at any time, an agreeable scent of various kinds. He may, at any time, meliorate his breathing air,—that main vehicle of vital power. Thus, by a proper application of the physical knowledge of our days, man may be kept in a perpetual serenity of mind, and if there is no incurable disease or defect in his organism, in constant vigor of health, and his life be prolonged beyond any parallel which present times afford."

"One or two persons are sufficient to direct the kitchen business. They have nothing else to do but to superintend the cookery, and to watch the time of the victuals being done, and then to remove them, with the table and vessels, into the dining-hall, or to the respective private apartments, by a slight motion of the hand at some crank. Any extraordinary desire of any person may be satisfied by going to the place where the thing is to be had; and anything that requires a particular preparation in cooking or baking, may be done by the person who desires it."

This is one of those instances in which the individual genius is found to consent, as indeed it always does, at last, with the universal. These last sentences have a certain sad and sober truth, which reminds us of the scripture of all nations. All expression of truth does at length take the deep ethical form. Here is hint of a place the most eligible of any in space, and of a servitor, in comparison with whom, all other helps dwindle into insignificance. We hope to hear more of him anon, for even crystal palace would be deficient without his invaluable services.

And as for the environs of the establishment,

"There will be afforded the most enrapturing views to be fancied, cut of the private apartments, from the galleries, from the roof, from its turrets and cupolas,—gardens as far as the eye can see, full of fruits and flowers, arranged in the most beautiful order, with walks, colonnades, aqueducts, canals, ponds, plains, amphitheatres, terraces, fountains, sculptural works, pavilions, gondolas, places for public amusement, etc., to delight the eye and fancy, the taste and smell." . . . "The walks and roads are to be paved with hard vitrified, large plates, so as to be always clean from all dirt in any weather or season. . . . The channels being of vitrified substance, and the water perfectly clear, and filtrated or distilled if required, may afford the most beautiful scenes imaginable, while a variety of fishes is seen clear down to the bottom playing about, and the canals may afford at the same time, the means of gliding smoothly along between various sceneries of art and nature, in beautiful gondolas, while their surface and borders may be covered with fine land and aquatic birds. The walks may be covered with porticos adorned with magnificent columns, statues and sculptural works; all of vitrified substance, and lasting for ever, while the beauties of nature around heighten the magnificence and deliciousness."

"The night affords no less delight to fancy and feelings. An infinite variety of grand, beautiful and fanciful objects and sceneries, radiating with crystalline brilliancy, by the illumination of gas-light; the human figures themselves, arrayed in the most beautiful pomp fancy may suggest, or the eye desire, shining even with brilliancy of stuffs and diamonds, like stones of various colors, elegantly shaped and arranged around the body; all reflected a thousand-fold in huge mirrors and reflectors of various forms; theatrical scenes of a grandeur and magnificence, and enrapturing illusions, unknown yet, in which any person may be either a spectator or actor; the speech and the songs reverberating with increased sound, rendered more sonorous and harmonious than by nature, by vaultings that are moveable into any shape at any time; the sweetest and most impressive harmony of music, produced by song and instruments partly not known yet, may thrill through the nerves and vary with other amusements and delights."

"At night the roof, and the inside and outside of the whole square, are illuminated by gas-light, which in the mazes of many-colored crystal-like colonnades and vaultings, is reflected with a brilliancy that gives to the whole a lustre of precious stones, as far as the eye can see,—such are the future abodes of men." . . . "Such is the life reserved to true intelligence, but withheld from ignorance, prejudice, and stupid adherence to custom." . . . "Such is the domestic life to be enjoyed by every human individual that will partake of it. Love and affection may there be fostered and enjoyed without any of the obstructions that oppose, diminish, and destroy them in the present state of men." . . . "It would be as ridiculous, then, to dispute and quarrel about the means of life, as it would be now about water to drink along mighty rivers, or about the permission to breathe air in the atmosphere, or about sticks in our extensive woods."

Thus is Paradise to be Regained, and that old and stern decree at length reversed. Man shall no more earn his living by the sweat of his brow. All labor shall be reduced to "a short turn of some crank," and "taking the finished article away." But there is a crank,—oh, how hard to be turned! Could there not be a crank upon a crank,—an infinitely small crank?— we would fain inquire. No,—alas! not. But there is a certain divine energy in every man, but sparingly employed as yet, which may be called the crank within,—the crank after all,—the prime mover in all machinery,—quite indispensable to all work. Would that we might get our hands on its handle! In fact no work can be shirked. It may be postponed indefinitely, but not infinitely. Nor can any really important work be made easier by co-operation or machinery. Not one particle of labor now threatening any man can be routed without being performed. It cannot be hunted out of the vicinity like jackals and hyenas. It will not run. You may begin by sawing the little sticks, or you may saw the great sticks first, but sooner or later you must saw them both.

We will not be imposed upon by this vast application of forces. We believe that most things will have to be accomplished still by the application called Industry. We are rather pleased after all to consider the small private, but both constant and accumulated force, which stands behind every spade in the field. This it is that makes the valleys shine, and the deserts really bloom. Sometimes, we confess, we are so degenerate as to reflect with pleasure on the days when men were yoked like cattle, and drew a crooked stick for a plough. After all, the great interests and methods were the same.

It is a rather serious objection to Mr. Etzler's schemes, that they require time, men, and money, three very superfluous and inconvenient things for an honest and well-disposed man to deal with. "The whole world," he tells us, "might therefore be really changed into a paradise, within less than ten years, commencing from the first year of an association for the purpose of constructing and applying the machinery." We are sensible of a startling incongruity when time and money are mentioned in this connection. The ten years which are proposed would be a tedious while to wait, if every man were at his post and did his duty, but quite too short a period, if we are to take time for it. But this fault is by no means peculiar to Mr. Etzler's schemes. There is far too much hurry and bustle, and too little patience and privacy, in all our methods, as if something were to be accomplished in centuries. The true reformer does not want time, nor money, nor co-operation, nor advice. What is time but the stuff delay is made of? And depend upon it, our virtue will not live on the interest of our money. He expects no income but our outgoes; so soon as we begin to count the cost the cost begins. And as for advice, the information floating in the atmosphere of society is as evanescent and unserviceable to him as gossamer for clubs of Hercules. There is absolutely no common sense; it is common nonsense. If we are to risk a cent or a drop of our blood, who then shall advise us? For ourselves, we are too young for experience. Who is old enough? We are older by faith than by experience. In the unbending of the arm to do the deed there is experience worth all the maxims in the world.

"It will now be plainly seen that the execution of the proposals is not proper for individuals. Whether it be proper for government at this time, before the subject has become popular, is a question to be decided; all that is to be done, is to step forth, after mature reflection, to confess loudly one's conviction, and to constitute societies. Man is powerful but in union with many. Nothing great, for the improvement of his own condition, or that of his fellow men, can ever be effected by individual enterprise."

Alas! this is the crying sin of the age, this want of faith in the prevalence of a man. Nothing can be effected but by one man. He who wants help wants everything. True, this is the condition of our weakness, but it can never be the means of our recovery. We must first succeed alone, that we may enjoy our success together. We trust that the social movements which we witness indicate an aspiration not to be thus cheaply satisfied. In this matter of reforming the world, we have little faith in corporations; not thus was it first formed.

But our author is wise enough to say, that the raw materials for the accomplishment of his purposes, are "iron, copper, wood, earth chiefly, and a union of men whose eyes and understanding are not shut up by preconceptions." Aye, this last may be what we want mainly,—a company of "odd fellows" indeed.

"Small shares of twenty dollars will be sufficient,"— in all, from "200,000 to 300,000,"—"to create the first establishment for a whole community of from 3000 to 4000 individuals"—at the end of five years we shall have a principal of 200 millions of dollars, and so paradise will be wholly regained at the end of the tenth year. But, alas, the ten years have already elapsed, and there are no signs of Eden yet, for want of the requisite funds to begin the enterprise in a hopeful manner. Yet it seems a safe investment. Perchance they could be hired at a low rate, the property being mortgaged for security, and, if necessary, it could be given up in any stage of the enterprise, without loss, with the fixtures.

Mr. Etzler considers this "Address as a touchstone, to try whether our nation is in any way accessible to these great truths, for raising the human creature to a superior state of existence, in accordance with the knowledge and the spirit of the most cultivated minds of the present time." He has prepared a constitution, short and concise, consisting of twenty-one articles, so that wherever an association may spring up, it may go into operation without delay; and the editor informs us that "Communications on the subject of this book may be addressed to C. F. Stollmeyer, No. 6, Upper Charles street, Northampton square, London."

But we see two main difficulties in the way. First, the successful application of the powers by machinery, (we have not yet seen the "Mechanical System,") and, secondly, which is infinitely harder, the application of man to the work by faith. This it is, we fear, which will prolong the ten years to ten thousand at least. It will take a power more than "80,000 times greater than all the men on earth could effect with their nerves," to persuade men to use that which is already offered them. Even a greater than this physical power must be brought to bear upon that moral power. Faith, indeed, is all the reform that is needed; it is itself a reform. Doubtless, we are as slow to conceive of Paradise as of Heaven, of a perfect natural as of a perfect spiritual world. We see how past ages have loitered and erred; "Is perhaps our generation free from irrationality and error? Have we perhaps reached now the summit of human wisdom, and need no more to look out for mental or physical improvement?" Undoubtedly, we are never so visionary as to be prepared for what the next hour may bring forth.

Μέλλει τὸ θεῖον δ'ἐστι τοιοῦτον φύσει.

The Divine is about to be, and such is its nature. In our wisest moments we are secreting a matter, which, like the lime of the shell fish, incrusts us quite over, and well for us, if, like it, we cast our shells from time to time, though they be pearl and of fairest tint. Let us consider under what disadvantages science has hitherto labored before we pronounce thus confidently on her progress.

"There was never any system in the productions of human labor; but they came into existence and fashion as chance directed men." "Only a few professional men of learning occupy themselves with teaching natural philosophy, chemistry, and the other branches of the sciences of nature, to a very limited extent, for very limited purposes, with very limited means." "The science of mechanics is but in a state of infancy. It is true, improvements are made upon improvements, instigated by patents of government; but they are made accidentally or at hap-hazard. There is no general system of this science, mathematical as it is, which developes its principles in their full extent, and the outlines of the application to which they lead. There is no idea of comparison between what is explored and what is yet to be explored in this science. The ancient Greeks placed mathematics at the head of their education. But we are glad to have filled our memory with notions, without troubling ourselves much with reasoning about them."

Mr. Etzler is not one of the enlightened practical men, the pioneers of the actual, who move with the slow deliberate tread of science, conserving the world; who execute the dreams of the last century, though they have no dreams of their own; yet he deals in the very raw but still solid material of all inventions. He has more of the practical than usually belongs to so bold a schemer, so resolute a dreamer. Yet his success is in theory, and not in practice, and he feeds our faith rather than contents our understanding. His book wants order, serenity, dignity, everything,— but it does not fail to impart what only man can impart to man of much importance, his own faith. It is true his dreams are not thrilling nor bright enough, and he leaves off to dream where he who dreams just before the dawn begins. His castles in the air fall to the ground, because they are not built lofty enough;

they should be secured to heaven's roof. After all, the theories and speculations of men concern us more than their puny execution. It is with a certain coldness and languor that we loiter about the actual and so called practical. How little do the most wonderful inventions of modern times detain us. They insult nature. Every machine, or particular application, seems a slight outrage against universal laws. How many fine inventions are there which do not clutter the ground? We think that those only succeed which minister to our sensible and animal wants, which bake or brew, wash or warm, or the like. But are those of no account which are patented by fancy and imagination, and succeed so admirably in our dreams that they give the tone still to our waking thoughts? Already nature is serving all those uses which science slowly derives on a much higher and grander scale to him that will be served by her. When the sunshine falls on the path of the poet, he enjoys all those pure benefits and pleasures which the arts slowly and partially realize from age to age. The winds which fan his cheek waft him the sum of that profit and happiness which their lagging inventions supply.

The chief fault of this book is, that it aims to secure the greatest degree of gross comfort and pleasure merely. It paints a Mahometan's heaven, and stops short with singular abruptness when we think it is drawing near to the precincts of the Christian's,—and we trust we have not made here a distinction without a difference. Undoubtedly if we were to reform this outward life truly and thoroughly, we should find no duty of the inner omitted. It would be employment for our whole nature; and what we should do thereafter would be as vain a question as to ask the bird what it will do when its nest is built and its brood reared. But a moral reform must take place first, and then the necessity of the other will be superseded, and we shall sail and plough by its force alone. There is a speedier way than the Mechanical System can show to fill up marshes, to drown the roar of the waves, to tame hyenas, secure agreeable environs, diversify the land, and refresh it with "rivulets of sweet water," and that is by the power of rectitude and true behavior. It is only for a little while, only occasionally, methinks, that we want a garden. Surely a good man need not be at the labor to level a hill for the sake of a prospect, or raise fruits and flowers, and construct floating islands, for the sake of a paradise. He enjoys better prospects than lie behind any hill. Where an angel travels it will be paradise all the way, but where Satan travels it will be burning marl and cinders. What says Veeshnoo Sarma? "He whose mind is at ease is possessed of all riches. Is it not the same to one whose foot is enclosed in a shoe, as if the whole surface of the earth were covered with leather?"

He who is conversant with the supernal powers will not worship these inferior deities of the wind, the waves, tide, and sunshine. But we would not disparage the importance of such calculations as we have described. They are truths in physics, because they are true in ethics. The moral powers no one would presume to calculate. Suppose we could compare the moral with the physical, and say how many horsepower the force of love, for instance, blowing on every square foot of a man's soul, would equal. No doubt we are well aware of this force; figures would not increase our respect for it; the sunshine is equal to but one ray of its heat. The light of the sun is but the shadow of love. "The souls of men loving and fearing God," says Raleigh, "receive influence from that divine light itself, whereof the sun's clarity, and that of the stars, is by Plato called but a shadow.

Lumen est umbra Dei, Deus est Lumen Luminis.
Light is the shadow of God's brightness, who is the
light of light," and, we may add, the heat of heat. Love
is the wind, the tide, the waves, the sunshine. Its
power is incalculable; it is many horse power. It
never ceases, it never slacks; it can move the globe
without a resting-place; it can warm without fire; it
can feed without meat; it can clothe without gar-
ments; it can shelter without roof; it can make a paradise within which will dispense with a paradise without. But though the wisest men in all ages have labored to publish this force, and every human heart
is, sooner or later, more or less, made to feel it, yet
how little is actually applied to social ends. True, it is
the motive power of all successful social machinery;
but, as in physics, we have made the elements do
only a little drudgery for us, steam to take the place
of a few horses, wind of a few oars, water of a few
cranks and hand-mills; as the mechanical forces have
not yet been generously and largely applied to make
the physical world answer to the ideal, so the power
of love has been but meanly and sparingly applied,
as yet. It has patented only such machines as the
almshouses, the hospital, and the Bible Society, while
its infinite wind is still blowing, and blowing down
these very structures, too, from time to time. Still less
are we accumulating its power, and preparing to act
with greater energy at a future time. Shall we not
contribute our shares to this enterprise, then?

Herald of Freedom *

WE have occasionally, for several years, met
with a number of this spirited journal, edited, as
abolitionists need not be informed, by Nathaniel P.
Rogers, once a counsellor at law in Plymouth, still
further up the Merrimack, but now, in his riper years,
come down the hills thus far, to be the Herald of
Freedom to those parts. We have been refreshed not a
little by the cheap cordial of his editorials, flowing like
his own mountain-torrents, now clear and sparkling,
now foaming and gritty, and always spiced with the
essence of the fir and the Norway pine; but never
dark nor muddy, nor threatening with smothered
murmurs, like the rivers of the plain. The effect of one
of his effusions reminds us of what the hydropathists
say about the electricity in fresh spring-water, compared with that which has stood over night to suit
weak nerves. We do not know of another notable and
public instance of such pure, youthful, and hearty
indignation at all wrong. The church itself must love
it, if it have any heart, though he is said to have dealt
rudely with its sanctity. His clean attachment to the
right, however, sanctions the severest rebuke we have
read.

We have neither room, nor inclination, to criticise
this paper, or its cause, at length, but would speak of
it in the free and uncalculating spirit of its author.
Mr. Rogers seems to us to occupy an honorable and
manly position in these days, and in this country,
making the press a living and breathing organ to
reach the hearts of men, and not merely "fine paper,
and good type," with its civil pilot sitting aft, and

* Herald of Freedom; published weekly by the New Hampshire Anti-Slavery Society: Concord, N. H. Vol. X. No. 4.

magnanimously waiting for the news to arrive,—the vehicle of the earliest news, but the *latest intelligence*, —recording the indubitable and last results, the marriages and deaths, alone. The present editor is wide awake, and standing on the beak of his ship; not as a scientific explorer under government, but a yankee sealer, rather, who makes those unexplored continents his harbors in which to refit for more adventurous cruises. He is a fund of news and freshness in himself,—has the gift of speech, and the knack of writing, and if anything important takes place in the Granite State, we may be sure that we shall hear of it in good season. No other paper that we know keeps pace so well with one forward wave of the restless public thought and sentiment of New England, and asserts so faithfully and ingenuously the largest liberty in all things. There is, beside, more unpledged poetry in his prose, than in the verses of many an accepted rhymer; and we are occasionally advertised by a mellow hunter's note from his trumpet, that, unlike most reformers, his feet are still where they should be, on the turf, and that he looks out from a serener natural life into the turbid arena of politics. Nor is slavery always a sombre theme with him, but invested with the colors of his wit and fancy, and an evil to be abolished by other means than sorrow and bitterness of complaint. He will fight this fight with what cheer may be. But to speak of his composition. It is a genuine yankee style, without fiction,—real guessing and calculating to some purpose, and reminds us occasionally, as does all free, brave, and original writing, of its great master in these days, Thomas Carlyle. It has a life above grammar, and a meaning which need not be parsed to be understood. But like those same mountain-torrents, there is rather too much slope to his channel, and the rainbow sprays and evaporations go double-quick-time to heaven, while the body of his water falls headlong to the plain. We would have more pause and deliberation, occasionally, if only to bring his tide to a head,—more frequent expansions of the stream, still, bottomless mountain tarns, perchance inland seas, and at length the deep ocean itself.

We cannot do better than enrich our pages with a few extracts from such articles as we have at hand. Who can help sympathizing with his righteous impatience, when invited to hold his peace or endeavor to convince the understandings of the people by well ordered arguments?

"Bandy *compliments* and *arguments* with the somnambulist, on 'table rock,' when all the waters of Lake Superior are thundering in the great horse-shoe, and deafening the very war of the elements! Would you not shout to him with a clap of thunder through a speaking-trumpet, if you could command it,—if possible to reach his senses in his appaling extremity! Did Jonah *argufy* with the city of Nineveh,—'yet forty days,' cried the vagabond prophet, 'and Nineveh shall be overthrown!' That was his salutation. And did the 'Property and Standing' turn up their noses at him, and set the mob on to him? Did the clergy *discountenance* him, and call him extravagant, misguided, a divider of churches, a disturber of parishes? What would have become of that city, if they had done this? Did they 'approve his *principles*' but dislike his *'measures'* and his *'spirit'* ! !

"Slavery must be cried down, denounced down, ridiculed down, and pro-slavery with it, or rather before it. Slavery will go when pro-slavery starts. The sheep will follow when the bell-wether leads. Down, then, with the bloody system, out of the land with it, and out of the world with it,—into the Red Sea with it. Men *sha'nt* be enslaved in this country any longer. Women and children *sha'nt* be flogged here any longer. If you undertake to hinder us, the worst is your own." . . . "But this is all fanaticism. *Wait and see.*"

He thus raises the anti-slavery 'war-whoop' in New Hampshire, when an important convention is to be held, sending the summons

"To none but the whole-hearted, fully-committed, cross-the-Rubicon spirits." . . . "From rich 'old Cheshire,' from Rockingham, with her horizon setting down away to the salt sea." . . . "From where the sun sets behind Kearsarge, even to where he rises gloriously over *Moses Norris's* own town of *Pittsfield*; and from Amoskeag to Ragged Mountains,—Coos—Upper Coos, home of the everlasting hills, send out your bold advocates of human rights,—wherever they lay, scattered by lonely lake, or Indian stream, or 'Grant,' or 'Location,'—from the trout-haunted brooks of the Amoriscoggin, and where the adventurous streamlet takes up its mountain march for the St. Lawrence.

"Scattered and insulated men, wherever the light of philanthropy and liberty has beamed in upon your solitary spirits, come down to us like your streams and clouds;—and our own Grafton,—all about among your dear hills, and your mountain-flanked valleys—whether you *home* along the swift Ammonoosuck, the cold Pemigewassett, or the ox-bowed Connecticut." . . .

"We are slow, brethren, dishonorably slow, in a cause like ours. Our feet should be as 'hinds' feet.' 'Liberty lies bleeding.' The leaden-colored wing of slavery obscures the land with its baleful shadow. Let us come together, and inquire at the hand of the Lord, what is to be done."

And again; on occasion of the New England Convention, in the Second-Advent Tabernacle, in Boston, he desires to try one more blast, as it were, 'on Fabyan's White Mountain horn.'

"Ho, then, people of the Bay State,—men, women, and children; children, women, and men, scattered friends of the *friendless*, wheresoever ye inhabit,—if habitations ye have, as such friends have not *always*,— along the sea-beat border of Old Essex and the Puritan Landing, and up beyond sight of the sea-cloud, among the inland hills, where the sun rises and sets upon the

dry land, in that vale of the Connecticut, too fair for
human content, and too fertile for virtuous industry,—
where deepens that haughtiest of earth's streams, on its
seaward way, proud with the pride of old Massachusetts. Are there any friends of the friendless negro
haunting such a valley as this? In God's name, I fear
there are none, or few, for the very scene looks apathy
and oblivion to the genius of humanity. I blow you the
summons though. Come, if any of you are there.

"And gallant little Rhode Island; *transcendent* abolitionists of the tiny commonwealth. I need not call
you. You are *called* the year round, and, instead of
sleeping in your tents, stand harnessed, and with
trumpets in your hands,—every one!

"Connecticut! yonder, the home of the Burleighs, the
Monroes, and the Hudsons, and the native land of old
George Benson! are you ready? 'All ready!'

"Maine here, off east, looking from my mountain
post, like an everglade. Where is your Sam. Fessenden,
who stood storm-proof 'gainst New Organization in '38?
Has he too much name as a jurist and an orator, to be
found at a New England Convention in '43? God for-
bid. Come one and all of you from 'Down East,' to
Boston, on the 30th, and let the sails of your coasters
whiten all the sea-road. Alas! there are scarce enough
of you to man a fishing boat. Come up, mighty in your
fewness.

"And green Vermont, what has become of your anti-
slavery host,—thick as your mountain maples,—master-
ing your very politics,—not by balance of power, but by
sturdy majority. Where are you now? Will you be at the
Advent Meeting on the 30th of May? Has anti-slavery
waxed too trying for your off-hand, how-are-ye, humanity? Have you heard the voice of Freedom of late?
Next week will answer.

"Poor, cold, winter-ridden New-Hampshire,—winter-
killed, I like to have said,—she will be there, bare-foot,
and bare-legged, making tracks like her old bloody-
footed volunteers at Trenton. She will be there, if she
can work her passage. I guess her minstrelsy* will,—
for birds can go independently of car, or tardy stage-
coach." . . .

* The Hutchinsons.

"Let them come as Macaulay says they did to the siege of Rome, when they did not leave old men and women enough to *begin* the harvests. Oh how few we should be, if every soul of us were there. How few, and yet it is the entire muster-roll of Freedom for all the land. We should have to beat up for recruits to complete the army of Gideon, or the *platoon* at the Spartan straits. The foe are like the grasshoppers for *multitude*, as for *moral power*. Thick grass mows the easier, as the Goth said of the enervated millions of falling Rome. They can't stand too thick, nor too tall for the anti-slavery scythe. Only be there at the mowing."

In noticing the doings of another Convention, he thus congratulates himself on the liberty of speech which anti-slavery concedes to all,—even to the Folsoms and Lamsons:—

"Denied a chance to speak elsewhere, because they are not mad after the fashion, they all flock to the anti-slavery boards as a kind of Asylum. And so the poor old enterprise has to father all the oddity of the times. It is a glory to anti-slavery, that she can allow the poor friends the right of speech. I hope she will always keep herself able to afford it. Let the constables wait on the State House, and Jail, and the *Meeting Houses*. Let the door-keeper at the Anti-Slavery Hall be that tall, celestial-faced Woman, that carries the flag on the National Standard, and says, 'without *concealment*,' as well as 'without compromise.' Let every body in, who has sanity enough to see the beauty of brotherly kindness, and let them say their fantasies, and magnanimously bear with them, seeing unkind pro-slavery drives them in upon *us*. We shall have *saner* and *sensibler* meetings then, than all others in the land put together."

More recently, speaking of the use which some of the clergy have made of Webster's plea in the Girard case, as a seasonable aid to the church, he proceeds:

"Webster is a great man, and the clergy run under his wing. They had better employ him as counsel against the Comeouters. He would'nt trust the defence

on the Girard will plea though, if they did. He would
not risk his fame on it, as a religious argument. He
would go and consult William Bassett, of Lynn, on the
principles of the 'Comeouters,' to learn their strength;
and he would get him a testament, and go into it as
he does into the Constitution, and after a year's study
of it he would hardly come off in the argument as he
did from the conflict with Carolina Hayne. On looking
into the case, he would advise the clergy not to go to
trial,—to settle,—or, if they could'nt to 'leave it out' to
a reference of 'orthodox deacons.' "

We will quote from the same sheet his indignant
and touching satire on the funeral of those public officers who were killed by the explosion on board the
Princeton, together with the President's slave; an accident which reminds us how closely slavery is linked
with the government of this nation. The President
coming to preside over a nation of *free* men, and the
man who stands *next to him a slave*!

"I saw account," says he, "of the burial of those
slaughtered politicians. The hearses passed along, of
Upshur, Gilmer, Kennon, Maxcy, and Gardner,—but
the dead slave, who fell in company with them on the
deck of the Princeton, was not there. He was held their
equal by the impartial gun-burst, but not allowed by the
bereaved nation a share in the funeral." . . . "Out upon
their funeral, and upon the paltry procession that went
in its train. Why did'nt they enquire for the body
of the *other man* who fell on that deck! And why has'nt
the nation inquired, and its press? I saw account of
the scene in a barbarian print, called the Boston Atlas,
and it was dumb on the absence of that body, as if
no such man had fallen. Why, I demand in the name
of human nature, was that sixth man of the game
brought down by that great shot, left unburied and
above ground,—for there is no account yet that his body
has been allowed the rites of sepulture." . . . "They
did'nt bury him even as a slave. They did'nt assign him
a jim-crow place in that solemn procession, that he
might follow to wait upon his enslavers in the land of
spirits. They have gone there without slaves or wait-

ers." . . . "The poor black man,—they enslaved and im-
bruted him all his life, and now he is dead, they have,
for aught appears, left him to decay and waste above
ground. Let the civilized world take note of the circumstance."

Such timely, pure, and unpremeditated expressions
of a public sentiment, such publicity of genuine indignation and humanity, as abound every where in
this journal, are the most generous gifts which a man
can make.

But since our voyage Rogers has died, and now
there is no one in New England to express the indignation or contempt which may still be felt at any
cant or inhumanity.

When, on a certain occasion, one said to him,
"Why do you go about as you do, agitating the community on the subject of abolition? Jesus Christ never
preached abolitionism:" he replied, "Sir, I have two
answers to your appeal to Jesus Christ. First, I deny
your proposition, that he never preached abolition.
That single precept of his—'Whatsoever ye would
that men should do to you, do ye even so to them'—
reduced to *practice*, would abolish slavery over the
whole earth in twenty-four hours. That is my first answer. I deny your proposition. Secondly, granting your
proposition to be true—and admitting what I deny—
that Jesus Christ did not preach the abolition of
slavery, then I say, *"he did'nt do his duty."*

His was not the wisdom of the head, but of the
heart. If perhaps he had all the faults, he had more
than the usual virtues of the radical. He loved his
native soil, her hills and streams, like a Burns or
Scott. As he rode to an antislavery convention, he
viewed the country with a poet's eye, and some of his
letters written back to his editorial substitute contain

as true and pleasing pictures of New England life and scenery as are anywhere to be found.

Whoever heard of Swamscot before? "Swamscot is all fishermen. Their business is all on the deep. Their village is ranged along the ocean margin, where their brave little fleets lay drawn up, and which are out at day-break on the mighty blue—where you may see them brooding at anchor—still and intent at their *profound* trade, as so many flies on the back of a wincing horse, and for whose wincings they care as little as the Swamscot Fishers heed the restless heavings of the sea around their barks. Every thing about savors of fish. Nets hang out on every enclosure. Flakes, for curing the fish are attached to almost every dwelling. Every body has a boat—and you'll see a huge pair of sea boots lying before almost every door. The air too savors strongly of the common finny vocation. Beautiful little beaches slope out from the dwellings into the Bay, all along the village—where the fishing boats lie keeled up, at low water, with their useless anchors hooked deep into the sand. A stranded bark is a sad sight—especially if it is above high water mark, where the next tide can't relieve it and set it afloat again. The Swamscot boats though, all look cheery, and as if sure of the next sea-flow. The people are said to be the freest in the region—owing perhaps to their bold and adventurous life. The Priests can't ride them *out into the deep*, as they can the shore folks."

His style and vein though often exaggerated and affected were more native to New England than those of any of her sons, and unfinished as his pieces were, yet their literary merit has been overlooked.

Wendell Phillips Before Concord Lyceum

CONCORD, MASS. MARCH 12TH, 1845.
Mr. Editor:

We have now, for the third winter, had our spirits refreshed, and our faith in the destiny of the commonwealth strengthened, by the presence and the eloquence of Wendell Phillips; and we wish to tender to him our thanks and our sympathy. The admission of this gentleman into the Lyceum has been strenuously opposed by a respectable portion of our fellow citizens, who themselves, we trust, whose descendants, at least, we know, will be as faithful conservers of the true order, whenever that shall be the order of the day,—and in each instance, the people have voted that they *would hear him*, by coming themselves and bringing their friends to the lecture room, and being very silent that they *might* hear. We saw some men and women, who had long ago *come out*, *going in* once more through the free and hospitable portals of the Lyceum; and many of our neighbors confessed, that they had had a 'sound season' this once.

It was the speaker's aim to show what the state, and above all the church, had to do, and now, alas! have done, with Texas and slavery, and how much, on the other hand, the individual should have to do with church and state. These were fair themes, and not mistimed; and his words were addressed to 'fit audience, *and not* few.'

We must give Mr. Phillips the credit of being a clean, erect, and what was once called a consistent man. He at least is not responsible for slavery, nor for American Independence; for the hypocrisy and superstition of the church, nor the timidity and selfishness of the state; nor for the indifference and willing ignorance of any. He stands so distinctly, so firmly, and so effectively, alone, and one honest man is so much more than a host, that we cannot but feel that he does himself injustice when he reminds us of 'the American Society, which he represents.' It is rare that we have the pleasure of listening to so clear and orthodox a speaker, who obviously has so few cracks or flaws in his moral nature—who, having words at his command in a remarkable degree, has much more than words, if these should fail, in his unquestionable earnestness and integrity—and, aside from their admiration at his rhetoric, secures the genuine respect of his audience. He unconsciously tells his biography as he proceeds, and we see him early and earnestly deliberating on these subjects, and wisely and bravely, without counsel or consent of any, occupying a ground at first, from which the varying tides of public opinion cannot drive him.

No one could mistake the genuine modesty and truth with which he affirmed, when speaking of the framers of the Constitution,—'I am wiser than they,' which with him has improved these sixty years' experience of its working; or the uncompromising consistency and frankness of the prayer which concluded, not like the Thanksgiving proclamations, with—'God save the Commonwealth of Massachusetts,' but God dash it into a thousand pieces, till there shall not remain a fragment on which a man can stand, and dare not tell his name—referring to the case of Frederick _____. To our disgrace we know not what to call him, unless Scotland will lend us the spoils of one of her Douglasses, out of history or fiction, for a season, till we be hospitable and brave enough to hear his proper name,—a fugitive slave in one more sense than we; who has proved himself the possessor of a

fair intellect, and has won a colorless reputation in
these parts; and who, we trust, will be as superior
to degradation from the sympathies of Freedom, as
from the antipathies of slavery. When, said Mr.
Phillips, he communicated to a New-Bedford audience, the other day, his purpose of writing his life,
and telling his name, and the name of his master,
and the place he ran from, the murmur ran round
the room, and was anxiously whispered by the sons of
the Pilgrims, 'He had better not!' and it was echoed
under the shadow of Concord monument, 'He had
better not!'

We would fain express our appreciation of the
freedom and steady wisdom, so rare in the reformer,
with which he declared that he was not born to
abolish slavery, but to do right. We have heard a few,
a very few, good political speakers, who afforded us
the pleasure of great intellectual power and acuteness,
of soldier-like steadiness, and of a graceful and
natural oratory; but in this man the audience might
detect a sort of moral principle and integrity, which
was more stable than their firmness, more discrimi-
nating than his own intellect, and more graceful than
his rhetoric, which was not working for temporary
or trivial ends. It is so rare and encouraging to listen
to an orator, who is content with another alliance
than with the popular party, or even with the sym-
pathising school of the martyrs, who can afford sometimes to be his own auditor if the mob stay away, and
hears himself without reproof, that we feel ourselves
in danger of slandering all mankind by affirming,
that here is one, who is at the same time an eloquent
speaker and a righteous man.

Perhaps, on the whole, the most interesting fact
elicited by these addresses, is the readiness of the
people at large, of whatever sect or party, to enter-

tain, with good will and hospitality, the most revolutionary and heretical opinions, when frankly and
adequately, and in some sort cheerfully, expressed.
Such clear and candid declaration of opinion served
like an electuary to whet and clarify the intellect of
all parties, and furnished each one with an additional
argument for that right he asserted.

We consider Mr. Phillips one of the most conspicuous and efficient champions of a true church and state
now in the field, and would say to him, and such as
are like him—'God speed you.' If you know of any
champion in the ranks of his opponents, who has
the valor and courtesy even of Paynim chivalry, if
not the Christian graces and refinement of this knight,
you will do us a service by directing him to these
fields forthwith, where the lists are now open, and
he shall be hospitably entertained. For as yet the
Red-cross knight has shown us only the gallant device upon his shield, and his admirable command
of his steed, prancing and curvetting in the empty
lists; but we wait to see who, in the actual breaking
of lances, will come tumbling upon the plain.

Resistance to Civil Government

I HEARTILY accept the motto,—"That government is best which governs least;" and I should like to see it acted up to more rapidly and systematically. Carried out, it finally amounts to this, which also I believe,—"That government is best which governs not at all;" and when men are prepared for it, that will be the kind of government which they will have. Government is at best but an expedient; but most governments are usually, and all governments are sometimes, inexpedient. The objections which have been brought against a standing army, and they are many and weighty, and deserve to prevail, may also at last be brought against a standing government. The standing army is only an arm of the standing government. The government itself, which is only the mode which the people have chosen to execute their will, is equally liable to be abused and perverted before the people can act through it. Witness the present Mexican war, the work of comparatively a few individuals using the standing government as their tool; for, in the outset, the people would not have consented to this measure.

This American government,—what is it but a tradition, though a recent one, endeavoring to transmit itself unimpaired to posterity, but each instant losing some of its integrity? It has not the vitality and force of a single living man; for a single man can bend it to his will. It is a sort of wooden gun to the people themselves; and, if ever they should use it in earnest as a real one against each other, it will surely split. But it is not the less necessary for this; for the people must have some complicated machinery or other, and hear its din, to satisfy that idea of government which they have. Governments show thus how successfully men can be imposed on, even impose on themselves, for their own advantage. It is excellent, we must all allow; yet this government never of itself furthered any enterprise, but by the alacrity with which it got out of its way. *It* does not keep the country free. *It* does not settle the West. *It* does not educate. The character inherent in the American people has done all that has been accomplished; and it would have done somewhat more, if the government had not sometimes got in its way. For government is an expedient by which men would fain succeed in letting one another alone; and, as has been said, when it is most expedient, the governed are most let alone by it. Trade and commerce, if they were not made of India rubber, would never manage to bounce over the obstacles which legislators are continually putting in their way; and, if one were to judge these men wholly by the effects of their actions, and not partly by their intentions, they would deserve to be classed and punished with those mischievous persons who put obstructions on the railroads.

But, to speak practically and as a citizen, unlike those who call themselves no-government men, I ask for, not at once no government, but *at once* a better government. Let every man make known what kind of government would command his respect, and that will be one step toward obtaining it.

After all, the practical reason why, when the power is once in the hands of the people, a majority are permitted, and for a long period continue, to rule, is not because they are most likely to be in the right, nor because this seems fairest to the minority, but because they are physically the strongest. But a gov-

ernment in which the majority rule in all cases cannot be based on justice, even as far as men understand it. Can there not be a government in which
majorities do not virtually decide right and wrong,
but conscience?—in which majorities decide only
those questions to which the rule of expediency is applicable? Must the citizen ever for a moment, or in the
least degree, resign his conscience to the legislator?
Why has every man a conscience, then? I think that
we should be men first, and subjects afterward. It is
not desirable to cultivate a respect for the law, so
much as for the right. The only obligation which I have
a right to assume, is to do at any time what I think
right. It is truly enough said, that a corporation has
no conscience; but a corporation of conscientious men
is a corporation *with* a conscience. Law never made
men a whit more just; and, by means of their respect
for it, even the well-disposed are daily made the
agents of injustice. A common and natural result of
an undue respect for law is, that you may see a file
of soldiers, colonel, captain, corporal, privates, pow-
der-monkeys and all, marching in admirable order
over hill and dale to the wars, against their wills, aye,
against their common sense and consciences, which
makes it very steep marching indeed, and produces
a palpitation of the heart. They have no doubt that
it is a damnable business in which they are concerned;
they are all peaceably inclined. Now, what are they?
Men at all? or small moveable forts and magazines, at
the service of some unscrupulous man in power?
Visit the Navy Yard, and behold a marine, such a man
as an American government can make, or such as it
can make a man with its black arts, a mere shadow
and reminiscence of humanity, a man laid out alive
and standing, and already, as one may say, buried

under arms with funeral accompaniments, though it
may be

> "Not a drum was heard, not a funeral note,
>   As his corse to the rampart we hurried;
> Not a soldier discharged his farewell shot
>   O'er the grave where our hero we buried."

The mass of men serve the State thus, not as men
mainly, but as machines, with their bodies. They are
the standing army, and the militia, jailers, constables,
posse comitatus, &c. In most cases there is no free
exercise whatever of the judgment or of the moral
sense; but they put themselves on a level with wood
and earth and stones, and wooden men can perhaps
be manufactured that will serve the purpose as well.
Such command no more respect than men of straw,
or a lump of dirt. They have the same sort of worth
only as horses and dogs. Yet such as these even are
commonly esteemed good citizens. Others, as most
legislators, politicians, lawyers, ministers, and office-
holders, serve the State chiefly with their heads; and,
as they rarely make any moral distinctions, they are
as likely to serve the devil, without intending it, as
God. A very few, as heroes, patriots, martyrs, reformers in the great sense, and *men*, serve the State with
their consciences also, and so necessarily resist it for
the most part; and they are commonly treated by it as
enemies. A wise man will only be useful as a man,
and will not submit to be "clay," and "stop a hole to
keep the wind away," but leave that office to his dust
at least: —

> "I am too high-born to be propertied,
>   To be a secondary at control,
>   Or useful serving-man and instrument
> To any sovereign state throughout the world."

He who gives himself entirely to his fellow-men
appears to them useless and selfish; but he who gives

himself partially to them is pronounced a benefactor and philanthropist.

How does it become a man to behave toward this American government to-day? I answer that he cannot without disgrace be associated with it. I cannot for an instant recognize that political organization as *my* government which is the *slave's* government also.

All men recognize the right of revolution; that is, the right to refuse allegiance to and to resist the government, when its tyranny or its inefficiency are great and unendurable. But almost all say that such is not the case now. But such was the case, they think, in the Revolution of '75. If one were to tell me that this was a bad government because it taxed certain foreign commodities brought to its ports, it is most probable that I should not make an ado about it, for I can do without them: all machines have their friction; and possibly this does enough good to counterbalance the evil. At any rate, it is a great evil to make a stir about it. But when the friction comes to have its machine, and oppression and robbery are organized, I say, let us not have such a machine any longer. In other words, when a sixth of the population of a nation which has undertaken to be the refuge of liberty are slaves, and a whole country is unjustly overrun and conquered by a foreign army, and subjected to military law, I think that it is not too soon for honest men to rebel and revolutionize. What makes this duty the more urgent is the fact, that the country so overrun is not our own, but ours is the invading army.

Paley, a common authority with many on moral questions, in his chapter on the "Duty of Submission to Civil Government," resolves all civil obligation into expediency; and he proceeds to say, "that so long as the interest of the whole society requires it, that is, so long as the established government cannot be resisted or changed without public inconveniency, it is the will of God that the established government be obeyed, and no longer." . . . "This principle being admitted, the justice of every particular case of resistance is reduced to a computation of the quantity of the danger and grievance on the one side, and of the probability and expense of redressing it on the other." Of this, he says, every man shall judge for himself. But Paley appears never to have contemplated those cases to which the rule of expediency does not apply, in which a people, as well as an individual, must do justice, cost what it may. If I have unjustly wrested a plank from a drowning man, I must restore it to him though I drown myself. This, according to Paley, would be inconvenient. But he that would save his life, in such a case, shall lose it. This people must cease to hold slaves, and to make war on Mexico, though it cost them their existence as a people.

In their practice, nations agree with Paley; but does any one think that Massachusetts does exactly what is right at the present crisis?

"A drab of state, a cloth-o'-silver slut,
    To have her train borne up, and her soul trail in the dirt."

Practically speaking, the opponents to a reform in Massachusetts are not a hundred thousand politicians at the South, but a hundred thousand merchants and farmers here, who are more interested in commerce and agriculture than they are in humanity, and are not prepared to do justice to the slave and to Mexico, *cost what it may.* I quarrel not with far-off foes, but with those who, near at home, co-operate with, and do the bidding of those far away, and without whom the latter would be harmless. We are accustomed to say, that the mass of men are unprepared; but improvement is slow, because the few are not materially wiser or better than the many. It is not so important that many should be as good as you, as that there be some absolute goodness somewhere; for that will leaven the whole lump. There are thousands who are *in opinion* opposed to slavery and to the war, who yet in effect do nothing to put an end to them; who, esteeming themselves children of Washington and Franklin, sit down with their hands in their pockets, and say that they know not what to do, and do nothing; who even postpone the question of freedom to the question of free-trade, and quietly read the prices-current along with the latest advices from Mexico, after dinner, and, it may be, fall asleep over them both. What is the price-current of an honest man and patriot to-day? They hesitate, and they regret, and sometimes they petition; but they do nothing in earnest and with effect. They will wait, well-disposed, for others to remedy the evil, that they may no longer have it to regret. At most, they give only a cheap vote, and a feeble countenance and God-speed, to the right, as it goes by them. There are nine hundred and ninety-nine patrons of virtue to one virtuous man; but it is easier to deal with the real possessor of a thing than with the temporary guardian of it.

All voting is a sort of gaming, like chequers or back-gammon, with a slight moral tinge to it, a playing with right and wrong, with moral questions; and betting naturally accompanies it. The character of the voters is not staked. I cast my vote, perchance, as I think right; but I am not vitally concerned that that right should prevail. I am willing to leave it to the majority. Its obligation, therefore, never exceeds that of expediency. Even voting *for the right* is *doing* nothing for it. It is only expressing to men feebly your desire that it should prevail. A wise man will not leave the right to the mercy of chance, nor wish it to prevail through the power of the majority. There is but little virtue in the action of masses of men. When the majority shall at length vote for the abolition of slavery, it will be because they are indifferent to slavery, or because there is but little slavery left to be abolished by their vote. *They* will then be the only slaves. Only *his* vote can hasten the abolition of slavery who asserts his own freedom by his vote.

I hear of a convention to be held at Baltimore, or elsewhere, for the selection of a candidate for the Presidency, made up chiefly of editors, and men who are politicians by profession; but I think, what is it to any independent, intelligent, and respectable man what decision they may come to, shall we not have the advantage of his wisdom and honesty, nevertheless? Can we not count upon some independent votes? Are there not many individuals in the country who do not attend conventions? But no: I find that the respectable man, so called, has immediately drifted from his position, and despairs of his country, when his country has more reason to despair of him. He forthwith adopts one of the candidates thus selected as the only *available* one, thus proving that he is himself *available* for any purposes of the demagogue. His vote is of no more worth than that of any unprincipled foreigner or hireling native, who may have been bought. Oh for a man who is a *man*, and, as my neighbor says, has a bone in his back which you cannot pass your hand through! Our statistics are at fault: the population has been returned too large. How many *men* are there to a square thousand miles in this country? Hardly one. Does not America offer any inducement for men to settle here? The American has dwindled into an Odd Fellow,—one who may be known by the development of his organ of gregariousness, and a manifest lack of intellect and cheerful self-reliance; whose first and chief concern, on coming into the world, is to see that the alms-houses are in good repair; and, before yet he has lawfully donned the virile garb, to collect a fund for the support of the widows and orphans that may be; who, in short, ventures to live only by the aid of the mutual insurance company, which has promised to bury him decently.

It is not a man's duty, as a matter of course, to devote himself to the eradication of any, even the most enormous wrong; he may still properly have other concerns to engage him; but it is his duty, at least, to wash his hands of it, and, if he gives it no thought longer, not to give it practically his support. If I devote myself to other pursuits and contemplations, I must first see, at least, that I do not pursue them sitting upon another man's shoulders. I must get off him first, that he may pursue his contemplations too. See what gross inconsistency is tolerated. I have heard some of my townsmen say, "I should like to have them order me out to help put down an insurrection of the slaves, or to march to Mexico,—see if I would go;" and yet these very men have each, directly by their allegiance, and so indirectly, at least, by their money, furnished a substitute. The soldier is applauded who refuses to serve in an unjust war by those who do not refuse to sustain the unjust government which makes the war; is applauded by those whose own act and authority he disregards and sets at nought; as if the State were penitent to that degree that it hired one to scourge it while it sinned, but not to that degree that it left off sinning for a moment. Thus, under the name of order and civil government, we are all made at last to pay homage to and support our own meanness. After the first blush of sin, comes its indifference and from immoral it becomes, as it were, *un*moral, and not quite unnecessary to that life which we have made.

The broadest and most prevalent error requires the most disinterested virtue to sustain it. The slight reproach to which the virtue of patriotism is commonly liable, the noble are most likely to incur. Those who, while they disapprove of the character and measures of a government, yield to it their allegiance and support, are undoubtedly its most conscientious supporters, and so frequently the most serious obstacles to reform. Some are petitioning the State to dissolve the Union, to disregard the requisitions of the President. Why do they not dissolve it themselves,—the union between themselves and the State,—and refuse to pay their quota into its treasury? Do not they stand in the same relation to the State, that the State does to the Union? And have not the same reasons prevented the State from resisting the Union, which have prevented them from resisting the State?

How can a man be satisfied to entertain an opinion merely, and enjoy *it*? Is there any enjoyment in it, if his opinion is that he is aggrieved? If you are cheated out of a single dollar by your neighbor, you do not rest satisfied with knowing that you are cheated, or with saying that you are cheated, or even with petitioning him to pay you your due; but you take effectual steps at once to obtain the full amount, and see that you are never cheated again. Action from principle,—the perception and the performance of right,—changes things and relations; it is essentially revolutionary, and does not consist wholly with any thing which was. It not only divides states and churches, it divides families; aye, it divides the *individual*, separating the diabolical in him from the divine.

Unjust laws exist: shall we be content to obey them,

or shall we endeavor to amend them, and obey them until we have succeeded, or shall we transgress them at once? Men generally, under such a government as this, think that they ought to wait until they have persuaded the majority to alter them. They think that, if they should resist, the remedy would be worse than the evil. But it is the fault of the government itself that the remedy *is* worse than the evil. *It* makes it worse. Why is it not more apt to anticipate and provide for reform? Why does it not cherish its wise minority? Why does it cry and resist before it is hurt? Why does it not encourage its citizens to be on the alert to point out its faults, and *do* better than it would have them? Why does it always crucify Christ, and excommunicate Copernicus and Luther, and pronounce Washington and Franklin rebels?

One would think, that a deliberate and practical denial of its authority was the only offence never contemplated by government; else, why has it not assigned its definite, its suitable and proportionate penalty? If a man who has no property refuses but once to earn nine shillings for the State, he is put in prison for a period unlimited by any law that I know, and determined only by the discretion of those who placed him there; but if he should steal ninety times nine shillings from the State, he is soon permitted to go at large again.

If the injustice is part of the necessary friction of the machine of government, let it go, let it go: perchance it will wear smooth,—certainly the machine will wear out. If the injustice has a spring, or a pulley, or a rope, or a crank, exclusively for itself, then perhaps you may consider whether the remedy will not be worse than the evil; but if it is of such a nature that it requires you to be the agent of injustice to another, then, I say, break the law. Let your life be a

counter friction to stop the machine. What I have to
do is to see, at any rate, that I do not lend myself to
the wrong which I condemn.

As for adopting the ways which the State has provided for remedying the evil, I know not of such ways.
They take too much time, and a man's life will be
gone. I have other affairs to attend to. I came into this
world, not chiefly to make this a good place to live in,
but to live in it, be it good or bad. A man has not every
thing to do, but something; and because he cannot do
every thing, it is not necessary that he should do
something wrong. It is not my business to be petitioning the governor or the legislature any more than it is
theirs to petition me; and, if they should not hear my
petition, what should I do then? But in this case the
State has provided no way: its very Constitution is the
evil. This may seem to be harsh and stubborn and
unconciliatory; but it is to treat with the utmost
kindness and consideration the only spirit that can
appreciate or deserves it. So is all change for the
better, like birth and death which convulse the body.

I do not hesitate to say, that those who call themselves abolitionists should at once effectually withdraw their support, both in person and property, from
the government of Massachusetts, and not wait till
they constitute a majority of one, before they suffer
the right to prevail through them. I think that it is
enough if they have God on their side, without waiting
for that other one. Moreover, any man more right
than his neighbors, constitutes a majority of one
already.

I meet this American government, or its representative the State government, directly, and face to face,
once a year, no more, in the person of its tax-gatherer;
this is the only mode in which a man situated as I am

necessarily meets it; and it then says distinctly, Recognize me; and the simplest, the most effectual, and, in the present posture of affairs, the indispensablest mode of treating with it on this head, of expressing your little satisfaction with and love for it, is to deny it then. My civil neighbor, the tax-gatherer, is the very man I have to deal with,—for it is, after all, with men and not with parchment that I quarrel,—and he has voluntarily chosen to be an agent of the government. How shall he ever know well what he is and does as an officer of the government, or as a man, until he is obliged to consider whether he shall treat me, his neighbor, for whom he has respect, as a neighbor and well-disposed man, or as a maniac and disturber of the peace, and see if he can get over this obstruction to his neighborliness without a ruder and more impetuous thought or speech corresponding with his action? I know this well, that if one thousand, if one hundred, if ten men whom I could name,—if ten *honest* men only,—aye, if *one* HONEST man, in this State of Massachusetts, *ceasing to hold slaves*, were actually to withdraw from this copartnership, and be locked up in the county jail therefor, it would be the abolition of slavery in America. For it matters not how small the beginning may seem to be: what is once well done is done for ever. But we love better to talk about it: that we say is our mission. Reform keeps many scores of newspapers in its service, but not one man. If my esteemed neighbor, the State's ambassador, who will devote his days to the settlement of the question of human rights in the Council Chamber, instead of being threatened with the prisons of Carolina, were to sit down the prisoner of Massachusetts, that State which is so anxious to foist the sin of slavery upon her sister,—though at present she can discover only an act of inhospitality to be the ground of a quarrel with her,—the Legislature would not wholly waive the subject the following winter.

Under a government which imprisons any unjustly, the true place for a just man is also a prison. The proper place to-day, the only place which Massachusetts has provided for her freer and less desponding spirits, is in her prisons, to be put out and locked out of the State by her own act, as they have already put themselves out by their principles. It is there that the fugitive slave, and the Mexican prisoner on parole, and the Indian come to plead the wrongs of his race, should find them; on that separate, but more free and honorable ground, where the State places those who are not *with* her but *against* her,—the only house in a slave-state in which a free man can abide with honor. If any think that their influence would be lost there, and their voices no longer afflict the ear of the State, that they would not be as an enemy within its walls, they do not know by how much truth is stronger than error, nor how much more eloquently and effectively he can combat injustice who has experienced a little in his own person. Cast your whole vote, not a strip of paper merely, but your whole influence. A minority is powerless while it conforms to the majority; it is not even a minority then; but it is irresistible when it clogs by its whole weight. If the alternative is to keep all just men in prison, or give up war and slavery, the State will not hesitate which to choose. If a thousand men were not to pay their tax-bills this year, that would not be a violent and bloody measure, as it would be to pay them, and enable the State to commit violence and shed innocent blood. This is, in fact, the definition of a peaceable revolution, if any such is possible. If the tax-gatherer, or any other public officer, asks me, as one has done, "But what shall I do?"

my answer is, "If you really wish to do any thing, resign your office." When the subject has refused allegiance, and the officer has resigned his office, then the revolution is accomplished. But even suppose blood should flow. Is there not a sort of blood shed when the conscience is wounded? Through this wound a man's real manhood and immortality flow out, and he bleeds to an everlasting death. I see this blood flowing now.

I have contemplated the imprisonment of the offender, rather than the seizure of his goods,—though both will serve the same purpose,—because they who assert the purest right, and consequently are most dangerous to a corrupt State, commonly have not spent much time in accumulating property. To such the State renders comparatively small service, and a slight tax is wont to appear exorbitant, particularly if they are obliged to earn it by special labor with their hands. If there were one who lived wholly without the use of money, the State itself would hesitate to demand it of him. But the rich man—not to make any invidious comparison—is always sold to the institution which makes him rich. Absolutely speaking, the more money, the less virtue; for money comes between a man and his objects, and obtains them for him; and it was certainly no great virtue to obtain it. It puts to rest many questions which he would otherwise be taxed to answer; while the only new question which it puts is the hard but superfluous one, how to spend it. Thus his moral ground is taken from under his feet. The opportunities of living are diminished in proportion as what are called the "means" are increased. The best thing a man can do for his culture when he is rich is to endeavour to carry out those schemes which he entertained when he was poor. Christ answered the Herodians according to their condition. "Show me the tribute-money," said he;—and one took a penny out of his pocket;—If you use money which has the image of Cæsar on it, and which he has made current and valuable, that is, *if you are men of the State*, and gladly enjoy the advantages of Cæsar's government, then pay him back some of his own when he demands it; "Render therefore to Cæsar that which is Cæsar's, and to God those things which are God's,"—leaving them no wiser than before as to which was which; for they did not wish to know.

When I converse with the freest of my neighbors, I perceive that, whatever they may say about the magnitude and seriousness of the question, and their regard for the public tranquillity, the long and the short of the matter is, that they cannot spare the protection of the existing government, and they dread the consequences of disobedience to it to their property and families. For my own part, I should not like to think that I ever rely on the protection of the State. But, if I deny the authority of the State when it presents its tax-bill, it will soon take and waste all my property, and so harass me and my children without end. This is hard. This makes it impossible for a man to live honestly and at the same time comfortably in outward respects. It will not be worth the while to accumulate property; that would be sure to go again. You must hire or squat somewhere, and raise but a small crop, and eat that soon. You must live within yourself, and depend upon yourself, always tucked up and ready for a start, and not have many affairs. A man may grow rich in Turkey even, if he will be in all respects a good subject of the Turkish government. Confucius said,—"If a State is governed by the principles of reason, poverty and misery are subjects of shame; if a State is not governed by the principles of reason, riches and honors are the subjects of shame."

No: until I want the protection of Massachusetts to be
extended to me in some distant southern port, where
my liberty is endangered, or until I am bent solely on
building up an estate at home by peaceful enterprise,
I can afford to refuse allegiance to Massachusetts, and
her right to my property and life. It costs me less in
every sense to incur the penalty of disobedience to the
State, than it would to obey. I should feel as if I were
worth less in that case.

Some years ago, the State met me in behalf of the
church, and commanded me to pay a certain sum
toward the support of a clergyman whose preaching
my father attended, but never I myself. "Pay it," it
said, "or be locked up in the jail." I declined to pay.
But, unfortunately, another man saw fit to pay it. I
did not see why the schoolmaster should be taxed to
support the priest, and not the priest the schoolmaster;
for I was not the State's schoolmaster, but I supported
myself by voluntary subscription. I did not see why
the lyceum should not present its tax-bill, and have
the State to back its demand, as well as the church.
However, at the request of the selectmen, I conde-
scended to make some such statement as this in
writing:—"Know all men by these presents, that I,
Henry Thoreau, do not wish to be regarded as a
member of any incorporated society which I have not
joined." This I gave to the town-clerk; and he has it.
The State, having thus learned that I did not wish to
be regarded as a member of that church, has never
made a like demand on me since; though it said that
it must adhere to its original presumption that time.
If I had known how to name them, I should then have
signed off in detail from all the societies which I never
signed on to; but I did not know where to find a
complete list.

I have paid no poll-tax for six years. I was put into

a jail once on this account, for one night; and, as I stood considering the walls of solid stone, two or three feet thick, the door of wood and iron, a foot thick, and the iron grating which strained the light, I could not help being struck with the foolishness of that institution which treated me as if I were mere flesh and blood and bones, to be locked up. I wondered that it should have concluded at length that this was the best use it could put me to, and had never thought to avail itself of my services in some way. I saw that, if there was a wall of stone between me and my townsmen, there was a still more difficult one to climb or break through, before they could get to be as free as I was. I did not for a moment feel confined, and the walls seemed a great waste of stone and mortar. I felt as if I alone of all my townsmen had paid my tax. They plainly did not know how to treat me, but behaved like persons who are underbred. In every threat and in every compliment there was a blunder; for they thought that my chief desire was to stand the other side of that stone wall. I could not but smile to see how industriously they locked the door on my meditations, which followed them out again without let or hinderance, and *they* were really all that was dangerous. As they could not reach me, they had resolved to punish my body; just as boys, if they cannot come at some person against whom they have a spite, will abuse his dog. I saw that the State was half-witted, that it was timid as a lone woman with her silver spoons, and that it did not know its friends from its foes, and I lost all my remaining respect for it, and pitied it.

Thus the State never intentionally confronts a man's sense, intellectual or moral, but only his body, his senses. It is not armed with superior wit or honesty, but with superior physical strength. I was not born to be forced. I will breathe after my own fashion. Let us see who is the strongest. What force has a multitude? They only can force me who obey a higher law than I. They force me to become like themselves. I do not hear of *men* being *forced* to live this way or that by masses of men. What sort of life were that to live? When I meet a government which says to me, "Your money or your life," why should I be in haste to give it my money? It may be in a great strait, and not know what to do: I cannot help that. It must help itself; do as I do. It is not worth the while to snivel about it. I am not responsible for the successful working of the machinery of society. I am not the son of the engineer. I perceive that, when an acorn and a chestnut fall side by side, the one does not remain inert to make way for the other, but both obey their own laws, and spring and grow and flourish as best they can, till one, perchance, overshadows and destroys the other. If a plant cannot live according to its nature, it dies; and so a man.

The night in prison was novel and interesting enough. The prisoners in their shirt-sleeves were enjoying a chat and the evening air in the door-way, when I entered. But the jailer said, "Come, boys, it is time to lock up;" and so they dispersed, and I heard the sound of their steps returning into the hollow apartments. My room-mate was introduced to me by the jailer, as "a first-rate fellow and a clever man." When the door was locked, he showed me where to hang my hat, and how he managed matters there. The rooms were whitewashed once a month; and this one, at least, was the whitest, most simply furnished, and probably the neatest apartment in the town. He naturally wanted to know where I came from, and what brought me there; and, when I had told him, I asked him in my turn how he came there, presuming him to be an honest man, of course; and, as the world goes, I believe he was. "Why," said he, "they accuse me of burning a barn; but I never did it." As near as I could discover, he had probably gone to bed in a barn when drunk, and smoked his pipe there; and so a barn was burnt. He had the reputation of being a clever man, had been there some three months waiting for his trial to come on, and would have to wait as much longer; but he was quite domesticated and contented, since he got his board for nothing, and thought that he was well treated.

He occupied one window, and I the other; and I saw, that, if one stayed there long, his principal business would be to look out the window. I had soon read all the tracts that were left there, and examined where former prisoners had broken out, and where a grate had been sawed off, and heard the history of the various occupants of that room; for I found that even here there was a history and a gossip which never circulated beyond the walls of the jail. Probably this is the only house in the town where verses are composed, which are afterward printed in a circular form, but not published. I was shown quite a long list of verses which were composed by some young men who had been detected in an attempt to escape, who avenged themselves by singing them.

I pumped my fellow-prisoner as dry as I could, for fear I should never see him again; but at length he showed me which was my bed, and left me to blow out the lamp.

It was like travelling into a far country, such as I had never expected to behold, to lie there for one night. It seemed to me that I never had heard the town-clock strike before, nor the evening sounds of the village; for we slept with the windows open, which were inside the grating. It was to see my native village in the light of the middle ages, and our Concord was turned into a Rhine stream, and visions of knights and castles passed before me. They were the voices of old burghers that I heard in the streets. I was an involuntary spectator and auditor of whatever was done and said in the kitchen of the adjacent village-inn,—a wholly new and rare experience to me. It was a closer view of my native town. I was fairly inside of it. I never had seen its institutions before. This is one of its peculiar institutions; for it is a shire town. I began to comprehend what its inhabitants were about.

In the morning, our breakfasts were put through the hole in the door, in small oblong-square tin pans, made to fit, and holding a pint of chocolate, with brown bread, and an iron spoon. When they called for the vessels again, I was green enough to return what bread I had left; but my comrade seized it, and said that I should lay that up for lunch or dinner. Soon after, he was let out to work at haying in a neighboring field, whither he went every day, and would not be back till noon; so he bade me good-day, saying that he doubted if he should see me again.

When I came out of prison,—for some one interfered, and paid the tax,—I did not perceive that great changes had taken place on the common, such as he observed who went in a youth, and emerged a tottering and gray-headed man; and yet a change had to my eyes come over the scene,—the town, and State, and country,—greater than any that mere time could effect. I saw yet more distinctly the State in which I lived. I saw to what extent the people among whom I lived could be trusted as good neighbors and friends; that their friendship was for summer weather only; that they did not greatly purpose to do right; that they were a distinct race from me by their prejudices and superstitions, as the Chinamen and Malays are; that, in their sacrifices to humanity, they ran no risks, not even to their property; that, after all, they were not so noble but they treated the thief as he had treated them, and hoped, by a certain outward observance and a few prayers, and by walking in a particular straight though useless path from time to time, to save their souls. This may be to judge my neighbors harshly; for I believe that most of them are not aware that they have such an institution as the jail in their village.

It was formerly the custom in our village, when a poor debtor came out of jail, for his acquaintances to salute him, looking through their fingers, which were crossed to represent the grating of a jail window, "How do ye do?" My neighbors did not thus salute me, but first looked at me, and then at one another, as if I had returned from a long journey. I was put into jail as I was going to the shoemaker's to get a shoe which was mended. When I was let out the next morning, I proceeded to finish my errand, and, having put on my mended shoe, joined a huckleberry party, who were impatient to put themselves under my conduct; and in half an hour,—for the horse was soon tackled,—was in the midst of a huckleberry field, on one of our highest hills, two miles off; and then the State was nowhere to be seen.

This is the whole history of "My Prisons."

I have never declined paying the highway tax, because I am as desirous of being a good neighbor as I am of being a bad subject; and, as for supporting schools, I am doing my part to educate my fellow-countrymen now. It is for no particular item in the tax-bill that I refuse to pay it. I simply wish to refuse allegiance to the State, to withdraw and stand aloof from it effectually. I do not care to trace the course of my dollar, if I could, till it buys a man, or a musket to shoot one with,—the dollar is innocent,—but I am concerned to trace the effects of my allegiance. In fact, I quietly declare war with the State, after my fashion, though I will still make what use and get what advantage of her I can, as is usual in such cases.

If others pay the tax which is demanded of me, from a sympathy with the State, they do but what they have already done in their own case, or rather they abet injustice to a greater extent than the State requires. If they pay the tax from a mistaken interest in the individual taxed, to save his property or prevent his going to jail, it is because they have not considered wisely how far they let their private feelings interfere with the public good.

This, then, is my position at present. But one cannot be too much on his guard in such a case, lest his action be biassed by obstinacy, or an undue regard for the opinions of men. Let him see that he does only what belongs to himself and to the hour.

I think sometimes, Why, this people mean well; they are only ignorant; they would do better if they knew how: why give your neighbors this pain to treat you as they are not inclined to? But I think, again, this is no reason why I should do as they do, or permit others to suffer much greater pain of a different kind. Again, I sometimes say to myself, When many millions of men, without heat, without ill-will, without personal feeling of any kind, demand of you a few shillings only, without the possibility, such is their constitution, of retracting or altering their present demand, and without the possibility, on your side, of appeal to any other millions, why expose yourself to this overwhelming brute force? You do not resist cold and hunger, the winds and the waves, thus obstinately; you quietly submit to a thousand similar necessities. You do not put your head into the fire. But just in proportion as I regard this as not wholly a brute force, but partly a human force, and consider that I have relations to those millions as to so many millions of men, and not of mere brute or inanimate things, I see that appeal is possible, first and instantaneously, from them to the Maker of them, and, secondly, from them to themselves. But, if I put my head deliberately into the fire, there is no appeal to fire or to the Maker of fire, and I have only myself to blame. If I could convince myself that I have any right to be satisfied with men as they are, and to treat them accordingly, and not according, in some respects, to my requisitions and expectations of what they and I ought to be, then, like a good Mussulman and fatalist, I should endeavor to be satisfied with things as they are, and say it is the will of God. And, above all, there is this difference between resisting this and a purely brute or natural force, that I can resist this with some effect; but I cannot expect, like Orpheus, to change the nature of the rocks and trees and beasts.

I do not wish to quarrel with any man or nation. I do not wish to split hairs, to make fine distinctions, or set myself up as better than my neighbors. I seek rather, I may say, even an excuse for conforming to the laws of the land. I am but too ready to conform to them. Indeed I have reason to suspect myself on this head; and each year, as the tax-gatherer comes round, I find myself disposed to review the acts and position of the general and state governments, and the spirit of the people, to discover a pretext for conformity. I believe that the State will soon be able to take all my work of this sort out of my hands, and then I shall be no better a patriot than my fellow-countrymen. Seen from a lower point of view, the Constitution, with all its faults, is very good; the law and the courts are very respectable; even this State and this American government are, in many respects, very admirable and rare things, to be thankful for, such as a great many have described them; but seen from a point of view a little higher, they are what I have described them; seen from a higher still, and the highest, who shall say what they are, or that they are worth looking at or thinking of at all?

However, the government does not concern me much, and I shall bestow the fewest possible thoughts on it. It is not many moments that I live under a government, even in this world. If a man is thought-free, fancy-free, imagination-free, that which *is not* never for a long time appearing *to be* to him, unwise rulers or reformers cannot fatally interrupt him.

I know that most men think differently from myself; but those whose lives are by profession devoted to the study of these or kindred subjects, content me as little as any. Statesmen and legislators, standing so completely within the institution, never distinctly and nakedly behold it. They speak of moving society,

but have no resting-place without it. They may be
men of a certain experience and discrimination, and
have no doubt invented ingenious and even useful
systems, for which we sincerely thank them; but all
their wit and usefulness lie within certain not very
wide limits. They are wont to forget that the world is
not governed by policy and expediency. Webster never
goes behind government, and so cannot speak with
authority about it. His words are wisdom to those
legislators who contemplate no essential reform in
the existing government; but for thinkers, and those
who legislate for all time, he never once glances at the
subject. I know of those whose serene and wise speculations on this theme would soon reveal the limits of
his mind's range and hospitality. Yet, compared with
the cheap professions of most reformers, and the still
cheaper wisdom and eloquence of politicians in general, his are almost the only sensible and valuable
words, and we thank Heaven for him. Comparatively,
he is always strong, original, and, above all, practical.
Still his quality is not wisdom, but prudence. The
lawyer's truth is not Truth, but consistency, or a
consistent expediency. Truth is always in harmony
with herself, and is not concerned chiefly to reveal the
justice that may consist with wrong-doing. He well
deserves to be called, as he has been called, the
Defender of the Constitution. There are really no
blows to be given by him but defensive ones. He is not
a leader, but a follower. His leaders are the men of
'87. "I have never made an effort," he says, "and
never propose to make an effort; I have never countenanced an effort, and never mean to countenance
an effort, to disturb the arrangement as originally
made, by which the various States came into the
Union." Still thinking of the sanction which the
Constitution gives to slavery, he says, "Because it was

a part of the original compact,—let it stand." Notwithstanding his special acuteness and ability, he is unable to take a fact out of its merely political relations, and behold it as it lies absolutely to be disposed of by the intellect,—what, for instance, it behoves a man to do here in America to-day with regard to slavery,—but ventures, or is driven, to make some such desperate answer as the following, while professing to speak absolutely, and as a private man,—from which what new and singular code of social duties might be inferred?—"The manner," says he, "in which the governments of those States where slavery exists are to regulate it, is for their own consideration, under their responsibility to their constituents, to the general laws of propriety, humanity, and justice, and to God. Associations formed elsewhere, springing from a feeling of humanity, or any other cause, have nothing whatever to do with it. They have never received any encouragement from me, and they never will."*

They who know of no purer sources of truth, who have traced up its stream no higher, stand, and wisely stand, by the Bible and the Constitution, and drink at it there with reverence and humility; but they who behold where it comes trickling into this lake or that pool, gird up their loins once more, and continue their pilgrimage toward its fountain-head.

No man with a genius for legislation has appeared in America. They are rare in the history of the world. There are orators, politicians, and eloquent men, by the thousand; but the speaker has not yet opened his mouth to speak, who is capable of settling the much-vexed questions of the day. We love eloquence for its own sake, and not for any truth which it may utter, or any heroism it may inspire. Our legislators have not

* These extracts have been inserted since the Lecture was read.

yet learned the comparative value of free-trade and of freedom, of union, and of rectitude, to a nation. They have no genius or talent for comparatively humble questions of taxation and finance, commerce and manufactures and agriculture. If we were left solely to the wordy wit of legislators in Congress for our guidance, uncorrected by the seasonable experience and the effectual complaints of the people, America would not long retain her rank among the nations. For eighteen hundred years, though perchance I have no right to say it, the New Testament has been written; yet where is the legislator who has wisdom and practical talent enough to avail himself of the light which it sheds on the science of legislation?

The authority of government, even such as I am willing to submit to,—for I will cheerfully obey those who know and can do better than I, and in many things even those who neither know nor can do so well,—is still an impure one: to be strictly just, it must have the sanction and consent of the governed. It can have no pure right over my person and property but what I concede to it. The progress from an absolute to a limited monarchy, from a limited monarchy to a democracy, is a progress toward a true respect for the individual. Is a democracy, such as we know it, the last improvement possible in government? Is it not possible to take a step further towards recognizing and organizing the rights of man? There will never be a really free and enlightened State, until the State comes to recognize the individual as a higher and independent power, from which all its own power and authority are derived, and treats him accordingly. I please myself with imagining a State at last which can afford to be just to all men, and to treat the individual with respect as a neighbor; which even would not think it inconsistent with its own repose, if a few were

to live aloof from it, not meddling with it, nor embraced by it, who fulfilled all the duties of neighbors
and fellow-men. A State which bore this kind of fruit,
and suffered it to drop off as fast as it ripened, would
prepare the way for a still more perfect and glorious
State, which also I have imagined, but not yet anywhere seen.

Slavery in Massachusetts

I LATELY attended a meeting of the citizens of Concord, expecting, as one among many, to speak on the subject of slavery in Massachusetts; but I was surprised and disappointed to find that what had called my townsmen together was the destiny of Nebraska, and not of Massachusetts, and that what I had to say would be entirely out of order. I had thought that the house was on fire, and not the prairie; but though several of the citizens of Massachusetts are now in prison for attempting to rescue a slave from her own clutches, not one of the speakers at that meeting expressed regret for it, not one even referred to it. It was only the disposition of some wild lands a thousand miles off, which appeared to concern them. The inhabitants of Concord are not prepared to stand by one of their own bridges, but talk only of taking up a position on the highlands beyond the Yellowstone river. Our Buttricks, and Davises, and Hosmers are retreating thither, and I fear that they will have no Lexington Common between them and the enemy. There is not one slave in Nebraska; there are perhaps a million slaves in Massachusetts.

They who have been bred in the school of politics fail now and always to face the facts. Their measures are half measures and make-shifts, merely. They put off the day of settlement indefinitely, and meanwhile, the debt accumulates. Though the Fugitive Slave Law had not been the subject of discussion on that occasion, it was at length faintly resolved by my townsmen, at an adjourned meeting, as I learn, that the compromise compact of 1820 having been repudiated by one of the parties, 'Therefore, . . . the Fugitive

Slave Law must be repealed.' But this is not the reason why an iniquitous law should be repealed. The fact which the politician faces is merely, that there is less honor among thieves than was supposed, and not the fact that they are thieves.

As I had no opportunity to express my thoughts at that meeting, will you allow me to do so here?

Again it happens that the Boston Court House is full of armed men, holding prisoner and trying a MAN, to find out if he is not really a SLAVE. Does any one think that Justice or God awaits Mr. Loring's decision? For him to sit there deciding still, when this question is already decided from eternity to eternity, and the unlettered slave himself, and the multitude around, have long since heard and assented to the decision, is simply to make himself ridiculous. We may be tempted to ask from whom he received his commission, and who he is that received it; what novel statutes he obeys, and what precedents are to him of authority. Such an arbiter's very existence is an impertinence. We do not ask him to make up his mind, but to make up his pack.

I listen to hear the voice of a Governor, Commander-in-Chief of the forces of Massachusetts. I hear only the creaking of crickets and the hum of insects which now fill the summer air. The Governor's exploit is to review the troops on muster days. I have seen him on horseback, with his hat off, listening to a chaplain's prayer. It chances that is all I have ever seen of a Governor. I think that I could manage to get along without one. If *he* is not of the least use to prevent my being kidnapped, pray of what important use is he likely to be to me? When freedom is most endangered, he dwells in the deepest obscurity. A distinguished clergyman told me that he chose the pro-

fession of a clergyman, because it afforded the most
leisure for literary pursuits. I would recommend to
him the profession of a Governor.

Three years ago, also, when the Simm's tragedy
was acted, I said to myself, there is such an officer,
if not such a man, as the Governor of Massachusetts,
—what has he been about the last fortnight? Has he
had as much as he could do to keep on the fence
during this moral earthquake? It seemed to me that
no keener satire could have been aimed at, no more
cutting insult have been offered to that man, than
just what happened—the absence of all inquiry after
him in that crisis. The worst and the most I chance to
know of him is, that he did not improve that opportunity to make himself known, and worthily known. He
could at least have *resigned* himself into fame. It appeared to be forgotten that there was such a man, or
such an office. Yet no doubt he was endeavoring to
fill the gubernatorial chair all the while. He was no
Governor of mine. He did not govern me.

But at last, in the present case, the Governor was
heard from. After he and the United States Government had perfectly succeeded in robbing a poor innocent black man of his liberty for life, and, as far as
they could, of his Creator's likeness in his breast, he
made a speech to his accomplices, at a congratulatory
supper!

I have read a recent law of this State, making it
penal for 'any officer of the Commonwealth' to 'detain, or aid in the . . . detention,' any where within
its limits, 'of any person, for the reason that he is
claimed as a fugitive slave.' Also, it was a matter of
notoriety that a writ of replevin to take the fugitive
out of the custody of the United States Marshal could
not be served, for want of sufficient force to aid the
officer.

I had thought that the Governor was in some sense
the executive officer of the State; that it was his business, as a Governor, to see that the laws of the State
were executed; while, as a man, he took care that he
did not, by so doing, break the laws of humanity; but
when there is any special important use for him, he
is useless, or worse than useless, and permits the
laws of the State to go unexecuted. Perhaps I do not
know what are the duties of a Governor; but if to be a
Governor requires to subject one's self to so much
ignominy without remedy, if it is to put a restraint
upon my manhood, I shall take care never to be
Governor of Massachusetts. I have not read far in the
statutes of this Commonwealth. It is not profitable
reading. They do not always say what is true; and
they do not always mean what they say. What I am
concerned to know is, that that man's influence and
authority were on the side of the slaveholder, and
not of the slave—of the guilty, and not of the innocent
—of injustice, and not of justice. I never saw him of
whom I speak; indeed, I did not know that he was
Governor until this event occurred. I heard of him
and Anthony Burns at the same time, and thus, undoubtedly, most will hear of him. So far am I from
being governed by him. I do not mean that it was any
thing to his discredit that I had not heard of him,
only that I heard what I did. The worst I shall say of
him is, that he proved no better than the majority of
his constituents would be likely to prove. In my opinion, he was not equal to the occasion.

The whole military force of the State is at the
service of a Mr. Suttle, a slaveholder from Virginia,
to enable him to catch a man whom he calls his
property; but not a soldier is offered to save a citizen
of Massachusetts from being kidnapped! Is this what
all these soldiers, all this *training* has been for these

seventy-nine years past? Have they been trained merely to rob Mexico, and carry back fugitive slaves to their masters?

These very nights, I heard the sound of a drum in our streets. There were men *training* still; and for what? I could with an effort pardon the cockerels of Concord for crowing still, for they, perchance, had not been beaten that morning; but I could not excuse this rub-a-dub of the 'trainers.' The slave was carried back by exactly such as these, i.e., by the soldier, of whom the best you can say in this connection is, that he is a fool made conspicuous by a painted coat.

Three years ago, also, just a week after the authorities of Boston assembled to carry back a perfectly innocent man, and one whom they knew to be innocent, into slavery, the inhabitants of Concord caused the bells to be rung and the cannons to be fired, to celebrate their liberty—and the courage and love of liberty of their ancestors who fought at the bridge. As if *those* three millions had fought for the right to be free themselves, but to hold in slavery three million others. Now-a-days, men wear a fool's cap, and call it a liberty cap. I do not know but there are some, who, if they were tied to a whipping-post, and could but get one hand free, would use it to ring the bells and fire the cannons, to celebrate *their* liberty. So some of my townsmen took the liberty to ring and fire; that was the extent of their freedom; and when the sound of the bells died away, their liberty died away also; when the powder was all expended, their liberty went off with the smoke.

The joke could be no broader, if the inmates of the prisons were to subscribe for all the powder to be used in such salutes, and hire the jailers to do the firing and ringing for them, while they enjoyed it through the grating.

This is what I thought about my neighbors.

Every humane and intelligent inhabitant of Concord, when he or she heard those bells and those cannons, thought not with pride of the events of the 19th of April, 1775, but with shame of the events of the 12th of April, 1851. But now we have half buried that old shame under a new one.

Massachusetts sat waiting Mr. Loring's decision, as if it could in any way affect her own criminality. Her crime, the most conspicuous and fatal crime of all, was permitting him to be the umpire in such a case. It was really the trial of Massachusetts. Every moment that she hesitated to set this man free—every moment that she now hesitates to atone for her crime, she is convicted. The Commissioner on her case is God; not Edward G. God, but simple God.

I wish my countrymen to consider, that whatever the human law may be, neither an individual nor a nation can ever commit the least act of injustice against the obscurest individual, without having to pay the penalty for it. A government which deliberately enacts injustice, and persists in it, will at length ever become the laughing-stock of the world.

Much has been said about American slavery, but I think that we do not even yet realize what slavery is. If I were seriously to propose to Congress to make mankind into sausages, I have no doubt that most of the members would smile at my proposition, and if any believed me to be in earnest, they would think that I proposed something much worse than Congress had ever done. But if any of them will tell me that to make a man into a sausage would be much worse,—would be any worse, than to make him into a slave,—than it was to enact the Fugitive Slave Law, I will accuse him of foolishness, of intellectual incapacity, of making a distinction without a difference. The one is just as sensible a proposition as the other.

I hear a good deal said about trampling this law under foot. Why, one need not go out of his way to do that. This law rises not to the level of the head or the reason; its natural habitat is in the dirt. It was born and bred, and has its life only in the dust and mire, on a level with the feet, and he who walks with freedom, and does not with Hindoo mercy avoid treading on every venomous reptile, will inevitably tread on it, and so trample it under foot,—and Webster, its maker, with it, like the dirt-bug and its ball.

Recent events will be valuable as a criticism on the administration of justice in our midst, or, rather, as showing what are the true resources of justice in any community. It has come to this, that the friends of liberty, the friends of the slave, have shuddered when they have understood that his fate was left to the legal tribunals of the country to be decided. Free men have no faith that justice will be awarded in such a case; the judge may decide this way or that; it is a kind of accident, at best. It is evident that he is not a competent authority in so important a case. It is no time, then, to be judging according to his precedents, but to establish a precedent for the future. I would much rather trust to the sentiment of the people. In their vote, you would get something of some value, at least, however small; but, in the other case, only the trammelled judgment of an individual, of no significance, be it which way it might.

It is to some extent fatal to the courts, when the people are compelled to go behind them. I do not wish to believe that the courts were made for fair weather, and for very civil cases merely,—but think of leaving it to any court in the land to decide whether more than three millions of people, in this case, a sixth part of a nation, have a right to be freemen or not! But it has been left to the courts of *justice*, so-called—to the Supreme Court of the land—and, as you all know, recognizing no authority but the Constitution, it has decided that the three millions are, and shall continue to be, slaves. Such judges as these are merely the inspectors of a pick-lock and murderer's tools, to tell him whether they are in working order or not, and there they think that their responsibility ends. There was a prior case on the docket, which they, as judges appointed by God, had no right to skip; which having been justly settled, they would have been saved from this humiliation. It was the case of the murderer himself.

The law will never make men free; it is men who have got to make the law free. They are the lovers of law and order, who observe the law when the government breaks it.

Among human beings, the judge whose words seal the fate of a man furthest into eternity, is not he who merely pronounces the verdict of the law, but he, whoever he may be, who, from a love of truth, and unprejudiced by any custom or enactment of men, utters a true opinion or *sentence* concerning him. He it is that *sentences* him. Whoever has discerned truth, has received his commission from a higher source than the chiefest justice in the world, who can discern only law. He finds himself constituted judge of the judge.—Strange that it should be necessary to state such simple truths.

I am more and more convinced that, with reference to any public question, it is more important to know what the country thinks of it, than what the city thinks. The city does not *think* much. On any moral question, I would rather have the opinion of

Boxboro than of Boston and New York put together.
When the former speaks, I feel as if somebody *had*
spoken, as if *humanity* was yet, and a reasonable
being had asserted its rights,—as if some unprejudiced
men among the country's hills had at length turned
their attention to the subject, and by a few sensible
words redeemed the reputation of the race. When, in
some obscure country town, the farmers come together to a special town meeting, to express their
opinion on some subject which is vexing the land,
that, I think, is the true Congress, and the most respectable one that is ever assembled in the United
States.

It is evident that there are, in this Commonwealth,
at least, two parties, becoming more and more distinct
—the party of the city, and the party of the country.
I know that the country is mean enough, but I am
glad to believe that there is a slight difference in her
favor. But as yet, she has few, if any organs, through
which to express herself. The editorials which she
reads, like the news, come from the sea-board. Let
us, the inhabitants of the country, cultivate self-re-
spect. Let us not send to the city for aught more essential than our broadcloths and groceries, or, if we
read the opinions of the city, let us entertain opinions
of our own.

Among measures to be adopted, I would suggest
to make as earnest and vigorous an assault on the
Press as has already been made, and with effect, on
the Church. The Church has much improved within
a few years; but the Press is almost, without exception, corrupt. I believe that, in this country, the press
exerts a greater and a more pernicious influence than
the Church did in its worst period. We are not a religious people, but we are a nation of politicians. We
do not care for the Bible, but we do care for the news-

paper. At any meeting of politicians,—like that at Concord the other evening, for instance,—how impertinent it would be to quote from the Bible! how pertinent to quote from a newspaper or from the Constitution! The newspaper is a Bible which we read every morning and every afternoon, standing and sitting, riding and walking. It is a Bible which every man carries in his pocket, which lies on every table and counter, and which the mail, and thousands of missionaries, are continually dispensing. It is, in short, the only book which America has printed, and which America reads. So wide is its influence. The editor is a preacher whom you voluntarily support. Your tax is commonly one cent daily, and it costs nothing for pew hire. But how many of these preachers preach the truth? I repeat the testimony of many an intelligent foreigner, as well as my own convictions, when I say, that probably no country was ever ruled by so mean a class of tyrants as, with a few noble exceptions, are the editors of the periodical press in *this* country. And as they live and rule only by their servility, and appealing to the worst, and not the better nature of man, the people who read them are in the condition of the dog that returns to his vomit.

The *Liberator* and the *Commonwealth* were the only papers in Boston, as far as I know, which made themselves heard in condemnation of the cowardice and meanness of the authorities of that city, as exhibited in '51. The other journals, almost without exception, by their manner of referring to and speaking of the Fugitive Slave Law, and the carrying back of the slave Simms, insulted the common sense of the country, at least. And, for the most part, they did this, one would say, because they thought so to secure the approbation of their patrons, not being aware that a sounder sentiment prevailed to any extent in the

heart of the Commonwealth. I am told that some of
them have improved of late; but they are still eminently time-serving. Such is the character they have
won.

But, thank fortune, this preacher can be even more
easily reached by the weapons of the reformer than
could the recreant priest. The free men of New England have only to refrain from purchasing and reading these sheets, have only to withhold their cents, to
kill a score of them at once. One whom I respect told
me that he purchased Mitchell's *Citizen* in the cars,
and then threw it out the window. But would not his
contempt have been more fatally expressed, if he had
not bought it?

Are they Americans? are they New Englanders?
are they inhabitants of Lexington, and Concord, and
Framingham, who read and support the Boston *Post*,
Mail, *Journal*, *Advertiser*, *Courier*, and *Times*? Are
these the Flags of our Union? I am not a newspaper
reader, and may omit to name the worst.

Could slavery suggest a more complete servility
than some of these journals exhibit? Is there any
dust which their conduct does not lick, and make
fouler still with its slime? I do not know whether the
Boston *Herald* is still in existence, but I remember to
have seen it about the streets when Simms was carried off. Did it not act its part well—serve its master
faithfully? How could it have gone lower on its belly?
How can a man stoop lower than he is low? do more
than put his extremities in the place of the head he
has? than make his head his lower extremity? When
I have taken up this paper with my cuffs turned up, I
have heard the gurgling of the sewer through every
column. I have felt that I was handling a paper
picked out of the public gutters, a leaf from the
gospel of the gambling-house, the groggery and the

brothel, harmonizing with the gospel of the Merchants' Exchange.

The majority of the men of the North, and of the South, and East, and West, are not men of principle. If they vote, they do not send men to Congress on errands of humanity, but while their brothers and sisters are being scourged and hung for loving liberty, while———I might here insert all that slavery implies and is,———it is the mismanagement of wood and iron and stone and gold which concerns them. Do what you will, O Government! with my wife and children, my mother and brother, my father and sister, I will obey your commands to the letter. It will indeed grieve me if you hurt them, if you deliver them to overseers to be hunted by hounds or to be whipped to death; but nevertheless, I will peaceably pursue my chosen calling on this fair earth, until perchance, one day, when I have put on mourning for them dead, I shall have persuaded you to relent. Such is the attitude, such are the words of Massachusetts.

Rather than do thus, I need not say what match I would touch, what system endeavor to blow up,—but as I love my life, I would side with the light, and let the dark earth roll from under me, calling my mother and my brother to follow.

I would remind my countrymen, that they are to be men first, and Americans only at a late and convenient hour. No matter how valuable law may be to protect your property, even to keep soul and body together, if it do not keep you and humanity together.

I am sorry to say, that I doubt if there is a judge in Massachusetts who is prepared to resign his office, and get his living innocently, whenever it is required of him to pass sentence under a law which is merely contrary to the law of God. I am compelled to see that they put themselves, or rather, are by character, in this respect, exactly on a level with the marine who discharges his musket in any direction he is ordered to. They are just as much tools and as little men. Certainly, they are not the more to be respected, because their master enslaves their understandings and consciences, instead of their bodies.

The judges and lawyers,—simply as such, I mean, —and all men of expediency, try this case by a very low and incompetent standard. They consider, not whether the Fugitive Slave Law is right, but whether it is what they call *constitutional*. Is virtue constitutional, or vice? Is equity constitutional, or iniquity? In important moral and vital questions like this, it is just as impertinent to ask whether a law is constitutional or not, as to ask whether it is profitable or not. They persist in being the servants of the worst of men, and not the servants of humanity. The question is not whether you or your grandfather, seventy years ago, did not enter into an agreement to serve the devil, and that service is not accordingly now due; but whether you will not now, for once and at last, serve God,—in spite of your own past recreancy, or that of your ancestor,—by obeying that eternal and only just CONSTITUTION, which He, and not any Jefferson or Adams, has written in your being.

The amount of it is, if the majority vote the devil to be God, the minority will live and behave accordingly, and obey the successful candidate, trusting that some time or other, by some Speaker's casting vote, perhaps, they may reinstate God. This is the highest principle I can get out of or invent for my neighbors. These men act as if they believed that they could safely slide down hill a little way—or a good way—and would surely come to a place, by and by, where they could begin to slide up again. This is expediency, or choosing that course which offers the

slightest obstacles to the feet, that is, a down-hill one.
But there is no such thing as accomplishing a righteous reform by the use of 'expediency.' There is no
such thing as sliding up hill. In morals, the only
sliders are backsliders.

Thus we steadily worship Mammon, both School,
and State, and Church, and the Seventh Day curse
God with a tintamar from one end of the Union to
the other.

Will mankind never learn that policy is not moral-
ity—that it never secures any moral right, but considers merely what is expedient? chooses the available
candidate, who is invariably the devil,—and what right
have his constituents to be surprised, because the
devil does not behave like an angel of light? What is
wanted is men, not of policy, but of probity—who
recognize a higher law than the Constitution, or the
decision of the majority. The fate of the country does
not depend on how you vote at the polls—the worst
man is as strong as the best at that game; it does
not depend on what kind of paper you drop into the
ballot-box once a year, but on what kind of man you
drop from your chamber into the street every morning.

What should concern Massachusetts is not the
Nebraska Bill, nor the Fugitive Slave Bill, but her own
slaveholding and servility. Let the State dissolve her
union with the slaveholder. She may wriggle and
hesitate, and ask leave to read the Constitution once
more; but she can find no respectable law or precedent which sanctions the continuance of such a
Union for an instant.

Let each inhabitant of the State dissolve his union
with her, as long as she delays to do her duty.

The events of the past month teach me to distrust
Fame. I see that she does not finely discriminate, but

coarsely hurrahs. She considers not the simple heroism of an action, but only as it is connected with its
apparent consequences. She praises till she is hoarse
the easy exploit of the Boston tea party, but will be
comparatively silent about the braver and more dis-
interestedly heroic attack on the Boston Court-House,
simply because it was unsuccessful!

Covered with disgrace, the State has sat down
coolly to try for their lives and liberties the men
who attempted to do its duty for it. And this is called
justice! They who have shown that they can behave
particularly well may perchance be put under bonds
for *their good behavior.* They whom truth requires
at present to plead guilty, are of all the inhabitants of
the State, pre-eminently innocent. While the Governor, and the Mayor, and countless officers of the
Commonwealth, are at large, the champions of liberty
are imprisoned.

Only they are guiltless, who commit the crime of
contempt of such a Court. It behoves every man to
see that his influence is on the side of justice, and let
the courts make their own characters. My sympathies
in this case are wholly with the accused, and wholly
against the accusers and their judges. Justice is sweet
and musical; but injustice is harsh and discordant.
The judge still sits grinding at his organ, but it yields
no music, and we hear only the sound of the handle.
He believes that all the music resides in the handle,
and the crowd toss him their coppers the same as
before.

Do you suppose that that Massachusetts which is
now doing these things,—which hesitates to crown
these men, some of whose lawyers, and even judges,
perchance, may be driven to take refuge in some poor
quibble, that they may not wholly outrage their in-
stinctive sense of justice,—do you suppose that she is

any thing but base and servile? that she is the champion of liberty?

Show me a free State, and a court truly of justice, and I will fight for them, if need be; but show me Massachusetts, and I refuse her my allegiance, and express contempt for her courts.

The effect of a good government is to make life more valuable,—of a bad one, to make it less valuable. We can afford that railroad, and all merely material stock, should lose some of its value, for that only compels us to live more simply and economically; but suppose that the value of life itself should be diminished! How can we make a less demand on man and nature, how live more economically in respect to virtue and all noble qualities, than we do? I have lived for the last month,—and I think that every man in Massachusetts capable of the sentiment of patriotism must have had a similar experience,—with the sense of having suffered a vast and indefinite loss. I did not know at first what ailed me. At last it occurred to me that what I had lost was a country. I had never respected the Government near to which I had lived, but I had foolishly thought that I might manage to live here, minding my private affairs, and forget it. For my part, my old and worthiest pursuits have lost I cannot say how much of their attraction, and I feel that my investment in life here is worth many per cent. less since Massachusetts last deliberately sent back an innocent man, Anthony Burns, to slavery. I dwelt before, perhaps, in the illusion that my life passed somewhere only *between* heaven and hell, but now I cannot persuade myself that I do not dwell *wholly within* hell. The site of that political organization called Massachusetts is to me morally covered with volcanic scoriæ and cinders, such as Milton de-

scribes in the infernal regions. If there is any hell
more unprincipled than our rulers, and we, the ruled,
I feel curious to see it. Life itself being worth less, all
things with it, which minister to it, are worth less.
Suppose you have a small library, with pictures to
adorn the walls—a garden laid out around—and contemplate scientific and literary pursuits, &c., and discover all at once that your villa, with all its contents,
is located in hell, and that the justice of the peace has
a cloven foot and a forked tail—do not these things
suddenly lose their value in your eyes?

I feel that, to some extent, the State has fatally interfered with my lawful business. It has not only
interrupted me in my passage through Court street
on errands of trade, but it has interrupted me and
every man on his onward and upward path, on which
he had trusted soon to leave Court street far behind.
What right had it to remind me of Court street? I have
found that hollow which even I had relied on for
solid.

I am surprised to see men going about their business as if nothing had happened. I say to myself—
Unfortunates! they have not heard the news. I am
surprised that the man whom I just met on horseback should be so earnest to overtake his newly-
bought cows running away—since all property is in-
secure—and if they do not run away again, they may
be taken away from him when he gets them. Fool!
does he not know that his seed-corn is worth less this
year—that all beneficent harvests fail as you approach
the empire of hell? No prudent man will build a stone
house under these circumstances, or engage in any
peaceful enterprise which it requires a long time to
accomplish. Art is as long as ever, but life is more
interrupted and less available for a man's proper pur-

suits. It is not an era of repose. We have used up all our inherited freedom. If we would save our lives, we must fight for them.

I walk toward one of our ponds, but what signifies the beauty of nature when men are base? We walk to lakes to see our serenity reflected in them; when we are not serene, we go not to them. Who can be serene in a country where both the rulers and the ruled are without principle? The remembrance of my country spoils my walk. My thoughts are murder to the State, and involuntarily go plotting against her.

But it chanced the other day that I scented a white water-lily, and a season I had waited for had arrived. It is the emblem of purity. It bursts up so pure and fair to the eye, and so sweet to the scent, as if to show us what purity and sweetness reside in, and can be extracted from, the slime and muck of earth. I think I have plucked the first one that has opened for a mile. What confirmation of our hopes is in the fragrance of this flower! I shall not so soon despair of the world for it, notwithstanding slavery, and the cowardice and want of principle of Northern men. It suggests what kind of laws have prevailed longest and widest, and still prevail, and that the time may come when man's deeds will smell as sweet. Such is the odor which the plant emits. If Nature can compound this fragrance still annually, I shall believe her still young and full of vigor, her integrity and genius unimpaired, and that there is virtue even in man, too, who is fitted to perceive and love it. It reminds me that Nature has been partner to no Missouri Compromise. I scent no compromise in the fragrance of the water-lily. It is not a *Nymphœa Douglassii*. In it, the sweet, and pure, and innocent, are wholly sundered from the obscene and baleful. I do not scent in this the time-serving irresolution of a Massachusetts

Governor, nor of a Boston Mayor. So behave that the odor of your actions may enhance the general sweetness of the atmosphere, that when we behold or scent a flower, we may not be reminded how inconsistent your deeds are with it; for all odor is but one form of advertisement of a moral quality, and if fair actions had not been performed, the lily would not smell sweet. The foul slime stands for the sloth and vice of man, the decay of humanity; the fragrant flower that springs from it, for the purity and courage which are immortal.

Slavery and servility have produced no sweet-scented flower annually, to charm the senses of men, for they have no real life: they are merely a decaying and a death, offensive to all healthy nostrils. We do not complain that they *live*, but that they do not *get buried*. Let the living bury them; even they are good for manure.

A Plea for Captain John Brown*

I TRUST that you will pardon me for being
here. I do not wish to force my thoughts upon you, but
I feel forced myself. Little as I know of Captain
Brown, I would fain do my part to correct the tone
and the statements of the newspapers, and of my
countrymen generally, respecting his character and
actions. It costs us nothing to be just. We can at
least express our sympathy with, and admiration of,
him and his companions, and that is what I now
propose to do.

First, as to his history.

I will endeavor to omit, as much as possible, what
you have already read. I need not describe his person
to you, for probably most of you have seen and will
not soon forget him. I am told that his grandfather,
John Brown, was an officer in the Revolution; that he
himself was born in Connecticut about the beginning
of this century, but early went with his father to Ohio.
I heard him say that his father was a contractor who
furnished beef to the army there, in the war of 1812;
that he accompanied him to the camp, and assisted
him in that employment, seeing a good deal of military life, more, perhaps, than if he had been a soldier,
for he was often present at the councils of the officers.
Especially, he learned by experience how armies are
supplied and maintained in the field—a work which,
he observed, requires at least as much experience and
skill as to lead them in battle. He said that few persons had any conception of the cost, even the pecuniary cost, of firing a single bullet in war. He saw

* Read to the citizens of Concord, Mass., Sunday Evening,
October 30, 1859. Also as the fifth lecture of the Fraternity
Course in Boston, November 1; and at Worcester, November 3.

enough, at any rate, to disgust him with a military life, indeed to excite in him a great abhorrence of it; so much so, that though he was tempted by the offer of some petty office in the army, when he was about eighteen, he not only declined that, but he also refused to train when warned, and was fined for it. He then resolved that he would never have anything to do with any war, unless it were a war for liberty.

When the troubles in Kansas began, he sent several of his sons thither to strengthen the party of the Free State men, fitting them out with such weapons as he had; telling them that if the troubles should increase, and there should be need of him, he would follow to assist them with his hand and counsel. This, as you all know, he soon after did; and it was through his agency, far more than any other's, that Kansas was made free.

For a part of his life he was a surveyor, and at one time he was engaged in wool-growing, and he went to Europe as an agent about that business. There, as every where, he had his eyes about him, and made many original observations. He said, for instance, that he saw why the soil of England was so rich, and that of Germany (I think it was) so poor, and he thought of writing to some of the crowned heads about it. It was because in England the peasantry live on the soil which they cultivate, but in Germany they are gathered into villages, at night. It is a pity that he did not make a book of his observations.

I should say that he was an old-fashioned man in his respect for the Constitution, and his faith in the permanence of this Union. Slavery he deemed to be wholly opposed to these, and he was its determined foe.

He was by descent and birth a New England farmer, a man of great common sense, deliberate and practical as that class is, and tenfold more so. He was like the best of those who stood at Concord Bridge once, on Lexington Common, and on Bunker Hill, only he was firmer and higher principled than any that I have chanced to hear of as there. It was no abolition lecturer that converted him. Ethan Allen and Stark, with whom he may in some respects be compared, were rangers in a lower and less important field. They could bravely face their country's foes, but he had the courage to face his country herself, when she was in the wrong. A Western writer says, to account for his escape from so many perils, that he was concealed under a "rural exterior;" as if, in that prairie land, a hero should, by good rights, wear a citizen's dress only.

He did not go to the college called Harvard, good old Alma Mater as she is. He was not fed on the pap that is there furnished. As he phrased it, "I know no more of grammar than one of your calves." But he went to the great university of the West, where he sedulously pursued the study of Liberty, for which he had early betrayed a fondness, and having taken many degrees, he finally commenced the public practice of Humanity in Kansas, as you all know. Such were *his humanities*, and not any study of grammar. He would have left a Greek accent slanting the wrong way, and righted up a falling man.

He was one of that class of whom we hear a great deal, but, for the most part, see nothing at all—the Puritans. It would be in vain to kill him. He died lately in the time of Cromwell, but he reappeared here. Why should he not? Some of the Puritan stock are said to have come over and settled in New England. They were a class that did something else than celebrate their forefathers' day, and eat parched corn in remembrance of that time. They were neither Democrats nor Republicans, but men of simple habits, straightforward, prayerful; not thinking much of rulers who did not fear God, not making many compromises, nor seeking after available candidates.

"In his camp," as one has recently written, and as I have myself heard him state, "he permitted no profanity; no man of loose morals was suffered to remain there, unless, indeed, as a prisoner of war. 'I would rather,' said he, 'have the small-pox, yellow fever, and cholera, all together in my camp, than a man without principle. . . . It is a mistake, sir, that our people make, when they think that bullies are the best fighters, or that they are the fit men to oppose these Southerners. Give me men of good principles,— God-fearing men,—men who respect themselves, and with a dozen of them I will oppose any hundred such men as these Buford ruffians.' " He said that if one offered himself to be a soldier under him, who was forward to tell what he could or would do, if he could only get sight of the enemy, he had but little confidence in him.

He was never able to find more than a score or so of recruits whom he would accept, and only about a dozen, among them his sons, in whom he had perfect faith. When he was here, some years ago, he showed to a few a little manuscript book,—his "orderly book" I think he called it,—containing the names of his company in Kansas, and the rules by which they bound themselves; and he stated that several of them had already sealed the contract with their blood. When some one remarked that, with the addition of a chaplain, it would have been a perfect Cromwellian troop, he observed that he would have been glad to add a chaplain to the list, if he could have found one who could fill that office worthily. It is easy enough to find one for the United States army. I believe that he had prayers in his camp morning and evening, nevertheless.

He was a man of Spartan habits, and at sixty was scrupulous about his diet at your table, excusing himself by saying that he must eat sparingly and fare hard, as became a soldier or one who was fitting himself for difficult enterprises, a life of exposure.

A man of rare common sense and directness of speech, as of action; a transcendentalist above all, a man of ideas and principles,—that was what distinguished him. Not yielding to a whim or transient impulse, but carrying out the purpose of a life. I noticed that he did not overstate any thing, but spoke within bounds. I remember, particularly, how, in his speech here, he referred to what his family had suffered in Kansas, without ever giving the least vent to his pent-up fire. It was a volcano with an ordinary chimney-flue. Also referring to the deeds of certain Border Ruffians, he said, rapidly paring away his speech, like an experienced soldier, keeping a reserve of force and meaning, "They had a perfect right to be hung." He was not in the least a rhetorician, was not talking to Buncombe or his constituents any where, had no need to invent any thing, but to tell the simple truth, and communicate his own resolution; therefore he appeared incomparably strong, and eloquence in Congress and elsewhere seemed to me at a discount. It was like the speeches of Cromwell compared with those of an ordinary king.

As for his tact and prudence, I will merely say, that at a time when scarcely a man from the Free States was able to reach Kansas by any direct route, at least without having his arms taken from him, he, carrying what imperfect guns and other weapons he could collect, openly and slowly drove an ox-cart through Missouri, apparently in the capacity of a surveyor, with his surveying compass exposed in it, and so passed unsuspected, and had ample opportunity to learn the designs of the enemy. For some time after his arrival he still followed the same profession. When, for instance, he saw a knot of the ruffians on the prairie, discussing, of course, the single topic which then occupied their minds, he would, perhaps, take his compass and one of his sons, and proceed to run an imaginary line right through the very spot on which that conclave had assembled, and when he came up to them, he would naturally pause and have some talk with them, learning their news, and, at last, all their plans perfectly; and having thus completed his real survey, he would resume his imaginary one, and run on his line till he was out of sight.

When I expressed surprise that he could live in Kansas at all, with a price set upon his head, and so large a number, including the authorities, exasperated against him, he accounted for it by saying, "It is perfectly well understood that I will not be taken." Much of the time for some years he has had to skulk in swamps, suffering from poverty and from sickness, which was the consequence of exposure, befriended only by Indians and a few whites. But though it might be known that he was lurking in a particular swamp, his foes commonly did not care to go in after him. He could even come out into a town where there were more Border Ruffians than Free State men, and transact some business, without delaying long, and yet not be molested; for said he, "No little handful of men were willing to undertake it, and a large body could not be got together in season."

As for his recent failure, we do not know the facts about it. It was evidently far from being a wild and desperate attempt. His enemy, Mr. Vallandigham, is compelled to say, thr t "it was among the best planned and executed conspiracies that ever failed."

Not to mention his other successes, was it a failure, or did it show a want of good management, to deliver from bondage a dozen human beings, and walk off with them by broad daylight, for weeks if not months, at a leisurely pace, through one State after another, for half the length of the North, conspicuous to all parties, with a price set upon his head, going into a court room on his way and telling what he had done, thus convincing Missouri that it was not profitable to try to hold slaves in his neighborhood?—and this, not because the government menials were lenient, but because they were afraid of him.

Yet he did not attribute his success, foolishly, to "his star," or to any magic. He said, truly, that the reason why such greatly superior numbers quailed before him, was, as one of his prisoners confessed, because they *lacked a cause*—a kind of armor which he and his party never lacked. When the time came, few men were found willing to lay down their lives in defence of what they knew to be wrong; they did not like that this should be their last act in this world.

But to make haste to *his* last act, and its effects.

The newspapers seem to ignore, or perhaps are really ignorant of the fact, that there are at least as many as two or three individuals to a town throughout the North, who think much as the present speaker does about him and his enterprise. I do not hesitate to say that they are an important and growing party. We aspire to be something more than stupid and timid chattels, pretending to read history and our bibles, but desecrating every house and every day we breathe in. Perhaps anxious politicians may prove that only seventeen white men and five negroes were concerned in the late enterprise, but their very anxiety to prove this might suggest to themselves that all is not told. Why do they still dodge the truth? They are so anxious because of a dim consciousness of the fact, which they do not distinctly face, that at least a million of the free inhabitants of the United States would have rejoiced if it had succeeded. They at most only criticise the tactics. Though we wear no crape, the thought of that man's position and probable fate is spoiling many a man's day here at the North for other thinking. If any one who has seen him here can pursue successfully any other train of thought, I do not know what he is made of. If there is any such who gets his usual allowance of sleep, I will warrant him to fatten easily under any circumstances which do not touch his body or purse. I put a piece of paper and a pencil under my pillow, and when I could not sleep, I wrote in the dark.

On the whole, my respect for my fellow-men, except as one may outweigh a million, is not being increased these days. I have noticed the cold-blooded way in which newspaper writers and men generally speak of this event, as if an ordinary malefactor, though one of unusual "pluck,"—as the Governor of Virginia is reported to have said, using the language of the cock-pit, "the gamest man he ever saw,"—had been caught, and were about to be hung. He was not dreaming of his foes when the governor thought he looked so brave. It turns what sweetness I have to gall, to hear, or hear of, the remarks of some of my neighbors. When we heard at first that he was dead, one of my townsmen observed that "he died as the fool dieth;" which, pardon me, for an instant suggested a likeness in him dying to my neighbor living. Others, craven-hearted, said disparagingly, that "he threw his life away," because he resisted the government. Which way have they thrown *their* lives, pray? —Such as would praise a man for attacking singly an ordinary band of thieves or murderers. I hear another ask, Yankee-like, "What will he gain by it?" as if he expected to fill his pockets by this enterprise. Such a one has no idea of gain but in this worldly sense. If it does not lead to a "surprise" party, if he does not get a new pair of boots, or a vote of thanks, it must be a failure. "But he won't gain any thing by it." Well, no, I don't suppose he could get four-and-sixpence a day for being hung, take the year round; but then he stands a chance to save a considerable part of his soul—and *such* a soul!—when *you* do not. No doubt you can get more in your market for a quart of milk than for a quart of blood, but that is not the market that heroes carry their blood to.

Such do not know that like the seed is the fruit, and that, in the moral world, when good seed is planted, good fruit is inevitable, and does not depend on our watering and cultivating; that when you plant, or bury, a hero in his field, a crop of heroes is sure to spring up. This is a seed of such force and vitality, that it does not ask our leave to germinate.

The momentary charge at Balaclava, in obedience to a blundering command, proving what a perfect machine the soldier is, has, properly enough, been celebrated by a poet laureate; but the steady, and for the most part successful charge of this man, for some years, against the legions of Slavery, in obedience to an infinitely higher command, is as much more memorable than that, as an intelligent and conscientious man is superior to a machine. Do you think that that will go unsung?

"Served him right"—"A dangerous man"—"He is undoubtedly insane." So they proceed to live their sane, and wise, and altogether admirable lives, reading their Plutarch a little, but chiefly pausing at that feat of Putnam, who was let down into a wolf's den; and in this wise they nourish themselves for brave and patriotic deeds some time or other. The Tract Society could afford to print that story of Putnam. You might open the district schools with the reading of it, for there is nothing about Slavery or the Church in it; unless it occurs to the reader that some pastors are *wolves* in sheep's clothing. "The American Board of Commissioners for Foreign Missions" even, might dare to protest against *that* wolf. I have heard of boards, and of American boards, but it chances that I never heard of this particular lumber till lately. And yet I hear of Northern men, women, and children, by families, buying a "life membership" in such societies as these;—a life-membership in the grave! You can get buried cheaper than that.

Our foes are in our midst and all about us. There is hardly a house but is divided against itself, for our foe is the all but universal woodenness of both head and heart, the want of vitality in man, which is the effect of our vice; and hence are begotten fear, superstition, bigotry, persecution, and slavery of all kinds. We are mere figure-heads upon a hulk, with livers in the place of hearts. The curse is the worship of idols, which at length changes the worshipper into a stone image himself; and the New Englander is just as much an idolater as the Hindoo. This man was an exception, for he did not set up even a political graven image between him and his God.

A church that can never have done with excommunicating Christ while it exists! Away with your broad and flat churches, and your narrow and tall churches! Take a step forward, and invent a new style of out-houses. Invent a salt that will save you, and defend our nostrils.

The modern Christian is a man who has consented to say all the prayers in the liturgy, provided you will let him go straight to bed and sleep quietly afterward. All his prayers begin with "Now I lay me down to sleep," and he is forever looking forward to the time when he shall go to his *long* rest." He has consented to perform certain old established charities, too, after a fashion, but he does not wish to hear of any new-fangled ones; he doesn't wish to have any supplementary articles added to the contract, to fit it to the present time. He shows the whites of his eyes on the Sabbath, and the blacks all the rest of the week. The evil is not merely a stagnation of blood, but a stagnation of spirit. Many, no doubt, are well disposed, but sluggish by constitution and by habit, and they cannot conceive of a man who is actuated by higher motives than they are. Accordingly they pronounce this man insane, for they know that *they* could never act as he does, as long as they are themselves.

We dream of foreign countries, of other times and races of men, placing them at a distance in history or space; but let some significant event like the present occur in our midst, and we discover, often, this distance and this strangeness between us and our nearest neighbors. *They* are our Austrias, and Chinas, and South Sea Islands. Our crowded society becomes well spaced all at once, clean and handsome to the eye, a city of magnificent distances. We discover why it was that we never got beyond compliments and surfaces with them before; we become aware of as many versts between us and them as there are between a wandering Tartar and a Chinese town. The thoughtful man becomes a hermit in the thoroughfares of the market-place. Impassable seas suddenly find their level between us, or dumb steppes stretch themselves out there. It is the difference of constitution, of intelligence, and faith, and not streams and mountains, that make the true and impassable boundaries between individuals and between states. None but the like-minded can come plenipotentiary to our court.

I read all the newspapers I could get within a week after this event, and I do not remember in them a single expression of sympathy for these men. I have since seen one noble statement, in a Boston paper, not editorial. Some voluminous sheets decided not to print the full report of Brown's words to the exclusion of other matter. It was as if a publisher should reject the manuscript of the New Testament, and print Wilson's last speech. The same journal which contained this pregnant news, was chiefly filled, in parallel columns, with the reports of the political conventions that were being held. But the descent to them was too steep. They should have been spared this contrast, been printed in an extra at least. To turn from the voices and deeds of earnest men to the *cackling* of political conventions! Office seekers and speech-makers, who do not so much as lay an honest egg, but wear their breasts bare upon an egg of chalk! Their great game is the game of straws, or rather that universal aboriginal game of the platter, at which the Indians cried *hub, bub!* Exclude the reports of religious and political conventions, and publish the words of a living man.

But I object not so much to what they have omitted as to what they have inserted. Even the *Liberator* called it "a misguided, wild, and apparently insane . . . effort." As for the herd of newspapers and magazines, I do not chance to know an editor in the country who will deliberately print anything which he knows will ultimately and permanently reduce the number of his subscribers. They do not believe that it would be expedient. How then can they print truth? If we do not say pleasant things, they argue, nobody will attend to us. And so they do like some travelling auctioneers, who sing an obscene song in order to draw a crowd around them. Republican editors, obliged to get their sentences ready for the morning edition, and accustomed to look at every thing by the twilight of politics, express no admiration, nor true sorrow even, but call these men "deluded fanatics"— "mistaken men"—"insane," or "crazed." It suggests what a *sane* set of editors we are blessed with, *not* "mistaken men"; who know very well on which side their bread is buttered, at least.

A man does a brave and humane deed, and at once, on all sides, we hear people and parties declaring, "I didn't do it, nor countenance *him* to do it, in any conceivable way. It can't be fairly inferred from my past career." I, for one, am not interested to hear you define your position. I don't know that I ever was, or ever shall be. I think it is mere egotism, or impertinent at this time. Ye needn't take so much pains to wash your skirts of him. No intelligent man will ever be convinced that he was any creature of yours. He went and came, as he himself informs us, "under the auspices of John Brown and nobody else." The Republican party does not perceive how many his *failure* will make to vote more correctly than they would have them. They have counted the votes of Pennsylvania &. Co., but they have not correctly counted Captain Brown's vote. He has taken the wind out of their sails, the little wind they had, and they may as well lie to and repair.

What though he did not belong to your clique! Though you may not approve of his method or his principles, recognize his magnanimity. Would you not like to claim kindredship with him in that, though in no other thing he is like, or likely, to you? Do you think that you would lose your reputation so? What you lost at the spile, you would gain at the bung.

If they do not mean all this, then they do not speak the truth, and say what they mean. They are simply at their old tricks still.

"It was always conceded to him," *says one who calls him crazy*, "that he was a conscientious man, very modest in his demeanor, apparently inoffensive, until the subject of Slavery was introduced, when he would exhibit a feeling of indignation unparalleled."

The slave-ship is on her way, crowded with its dying victims; new cargoes are being added in mid ocean; a small crew of slaveholders, countenanced by a large body of passengers, is smothering four millions under the hatches, and yet the politician asserts that the only proper way by which deliverance is to be obtained, is by "the quiet diffusion of the sentiments of humanity," without any "outbreak." As if the sentiments of humanity were ever found unaccompanied by its deeds, and you could disperse them, all finished to order, the pure article, as easily as water with a watering-pot, and so lay the dust. What is that that I hear cast overboard? The bodies of the dead that have found deliverance. That is the way we are "diffusing" humanity, and its sentiments with it.

Prominent and influential editors, accustomed to deal with politicians, men of an infinitely lower grade, say, in their ignorance, that he acted "on the principle of revenge." They do not know the man. They must enlarge themselves to conceive of him. I have no doubt that the time will come when they will begin to see him as he was. They have got to conceive of a man of faith and of religious principle, and not a politician or an Indian; of a man who did not wait till he was personally interfered with, or thwarted in some harmless business, before he gave his life to the cause of the oppressed.

If Walker may be considered the representative of the South, I wish I could say that Brown was the representative of the North. He was a superior man. He did not value his bodily life in comparison with ideal things. He did not recognize unjust human laws, but resisted them as he was bid. For once we are lifted out of the trivialness and dust of politics into the region of truth and manhood. No man in America has ever stood up so persistently and effectively for the dignity of human nature, knowing himself for a man, and the equal of any and all governments. In that sense he was the most American of us all. He needed no babbling lawyer, making false issues, to defend him. He was more than a match for all the judges that American voters, or office-holders of whatever grade, can create. He could not have been tried by a jury of his peers, because his peers did not exist. When a man stands up serenely against the condemnation and vengeance of mankind, rising above them literally *by a whole body*,—even though he were of late the vilest murderer, who has settled that matter with himself,—the spectacle is a sublime one,—didn't ye know it, ye Liberators, ye Tribunes, ye Republicans?—and we become criminal in comparison. Do yourselves the honor to recognize him. He needs none of your respect.

As for the Democratic journals, they are not human enough to affect me at all. I do not feel indignation at any thing they may say.

I am aware that I anticipate a little, that he was still, at the last accounts, alive in the hands of his foes; but that being the case, I have all along found myself thinking and speaking of him as physically dead.

I do not believe in erecting statues to those who still live in our hearts, whose bones have not yet crumbled in the earth around us, but I would rather see the statue of Captain Brown in the Massachusetts State-House yard, than that of any other man whom I know. I rejoice that I live in this age—that I am his contemporary.

What a contrast, when we turn to that political party which is so anxiously shuffling him and his plot out of its way, and looking around for some available slaveholder, perhaps, to be its candidate, at least for one who will execute the Fugitive Slave Law, and all those other unjust laws which he took up arms to annul!

Insane! A father and six sons, and one son-in-law, and several more men besides,—as many at least as twelve disciples,—all struck with insanity at once; while the sane tyrant holds with a firmer gripe than ever his four millions of slaves, and a thousand sane editors, his abettors, are saving their country and their bacon! Just as insane were his efforts in Kansas. Ask the tyrant who is his most dangerous foe, the sane man or the insane. Do the thousands who know him best, who have rejoiced at his deeds in Kansas, and have afforded him material aid there, think him insane? Such a use of this word is a mere trope with most who persist in using it, and I have no doubt that many of the rest have already in silence retracted their words.

Read his admirable answers to Mason and others. How they are dwarfed and defeated by the contrast! On the one side, half brutish, half timid questioning; on the other, truth, clear as lightning, crashing into their obscene temples. They are made to stand with Pilate, and Gessler, and the Inquisition. How ineffectual their speech and action! and what a void their silence! They are but helpless tools in this great work. It was no human power that gathered them about this preacher.

What have Massachusetts and the North sent a few *sane* representatives to Congress for, of late years?— to declare with effect what kind of sentiments? All their speeches put together and boiled down,—and probably they themselves will confess it,—do not match for manly directness and force, and for simple truth, the few casual remarks of crazy John Brown, on the floor of the Harper's Ferry engine house;— that man whom you are about to hang, to send to the other world, though not to represent *you* there. No, he was not our representative in any sense. He was too fair a specimen of a man to represent the like of us. Who, then, *were* his constituents? If you read his words understandingly you will find out. In his case there is no idle eloquence, no made, nor maiden speech, no compliments to the oppressor. Truth is his inspirer, and earnestness the polisher of his sentences. He could afford to lose his Sharps' rifles, while he retained his faculty of speech, a Sharps' rifle of infinitely surer and longer range.

And the *New York Herald* reports the conversation "*verbatim*"! It does not know of what undying words it is made the vehicle.

I have no respect for the penetration of any man who can read the report of that conversation, and still call the principal in it insane. It has the ring of a saner sanity than an ordinary discipline and habits of life, than an ordinary organization, secure. Take any sentence of it—"Any questions that I can honorably answer, I will; not otherwise. So far as I am myself concerned, I have told every thing truthfully. I value my word, sir." The few who talk about his vindictive spirit, while they really admire his heroism, have no test by which to detect a noble man, no amalgam to combine with his pure gold. They mix their own dross with it.

It is a relief to turn from these slanders to the testimony of his more truthful, but frightened, jailers and hangmen. Governor Wise speaks far more justly and appreciatingly of him than any Northern editor, or politician, or public personage, that I chance to have heard from. I know that you can afford to hear him again on this subject. He says: "They are themselves mistaken who take him to be a madman. . . . He is cool, collected, and indomitable, and it is but just to him to say, that he was humane to his prisoners. . . . And he inspired me with great trust in his integrity as a man of truth. He is a fanatic, vain and garrulous," (I leave that part to Mr. Wise) "but firm, truthful, and intelligent. His men, too, who survive, are like him. . . . Colonel Washington says that he was the coolest and firmest man he ever saw in defying danger and death. With one son dead by his side, and another shot through, he felt the pulse of his dying son with one hand, and held his rifle with the other, and commanded his men with the utmost composure, encouraging them to be firm, and to sell their lives as dear as they could. Of the three white prisoners, Brown, Stevens, and Coppoc, it was hard to say which was most firm. . . ."

Almost the first Northern men whom the slaveholder has learned to respect!

The testimony of Mr. Vallandigham, though less valuable, is of the same purport, that "it is vain to underrate either the man or his conspiracy. . . . He is the farthest possible remove from the ordinary ruffian, fanatic, or madman."

"All is quiet at Harper's Ferry," say the journals. What is the character of that calm which follows when the law and the slaveholder prevail? I regard this event as a touchstone designed to bring out, with glaring distinctness, the character of this government. We needed to be thus assisted to see it by the light of history. It needed to see itself. When a government puts forth its strength on the side of injustice, as ours to maintain Slavery and kill the liberators of the slave, it reveals itself a merely brute force, or worse, a demoniacal force. It is the head of the Plug Uglies. It is more manifest than ever that tyranny rules. I see this government to be effectually allied with France and Austria in oppressing mankind. There sits a tyrant holding fettered four millions of slaves; here comes their heroic liberator. This most hypocritical and diabolical government looks up from its seat on the gasping four millions, and inquires with an assumption of innocence, "What do you assault me for? Am I not an honest man? Cease agitation on this subject, or I will make a slave of you, too, or else hang you."

We talk about a *representative* government; but what a monster of a government is that where the noblest faculties of the mind, and the *whole* heart, are not *represented*. A semi-human tiger or ox, stalking over the earth, with its heart taken out and the top of its brain shot away. Heroes have fought well on their stumps when their legs were shot off, but I never heard of any good done by such a government as that.

The only government that I recognize,—and it matters not how few are at the head of it, or how small its army,—is that power that establishes justice in the land, never that which establishes injustice. What shall we think of a government to which all the truly brave and just men in the land are enemies, standing between it and those whom it oppresses? A government that pretends to be Christian and crucifies a million Christs every day!

Treason! Where does such treason take its rise? I cannot help thinking of you as you deserve, ye governments. Can you dry up the fountains of thought? High treason, when it is resistance to tyranny here below, has its origin in, and is first committed by the power that makes and forever recreates man. When you have caught and hung all these human rebels, you have accomplished nothing but your own guilt, for you have not struck at the fountain head. You presume to contend with a foe against whom West Point cadets and rifled cannon *point* not. Can all the art of the cannon-founder tempt matter to turn against its maker? Is the form in which the founder thinks he casts it more essential than the constitution of it and of himself?

The United States have a coffle of four millions of slaves. They are determined to keep them in this condition; and Massachusetts is one of the confederated overseers to prevent their escape. Such are not all the inhabitants of Massachusetts, but such are they who rule and are obeyed here. It was Massachusetts, as well as Virginia, that put down this insurrection at Harper's Ferry. She sent the marines there, and she will have to pay the penalty of her sin.

Suppose that there is a society in this State that out of its own purse and magnanimity saves all the fugitive slaves that run to us, and protects our colored fellow-citizens, and leaves the other work to the Government, so-called. Is not that government fast losing its occupation, and becoming contemptible to mankind? If private men are obliged to perform the offices of government, to protect the weak and dispense justice, then the government becomes only a hired man, or clerk, to perform menial or indifferent

services. Of course, that is but the shadow of a government whose existence necessitates a Vigilant Committee. What should we think of the oriental Cadi
even, behind whom worked in secret a Vigilant Committee? But such is the character of our Northern
States generally; each has its Vigilant Committee.
And, to a certain extent, these crazy governments
recognize and accept this relation. They say, virtually,
"We'll be glad to work for you on these terms, only
don't make a noise about it." And thus the government, its salary being insured, withdraws into the
back shop, taking the constitution with it, and be-
stows most of its labor on repairing that. When I
hear it at work sometimes, as I go by, it reminds me,
at best, of those farmers who in winter contrive to
turn a penny by following the coopering business.
And what kind of spirit is their barrel made to hold?
They speculate in stocks, and bore holes in mountains, but they are not competent to lay out even a
decent highway. The only *free* road, the Underground
Railroad, is owned and managed by the Vigilant
Committee. *They* have tunnelled under the whole
breadth of the land. Such a government is losing its
power and respectability as surely as water runs out
of a leaky vessel, and is held by one that can contain
it.

I hear many condemn these men because they
were so few. When were the good and the brave ever
in a majority? Would you have had him wait till that
time came?—till you and I came over to him? The very
fact that he had no rabble or troop of hirelings about
him would alone distinguish him from ordinary
heroes. His company was small indeed, because few
could be found worthy to pass muster. Each one who
there laid down his life for the poor and oppressed,
was a picked man, called out of many thousands, if not

millions; apparently a man of principle, of rare courage and devoted humanity, ready to sacrifice his life at
any moment for the benefit of his fellow man. It may
be doubted if there were as many more their equals
in these respects in all the country—I speak of his
followers only—for their leader, no doubt, scoured the
land far and wide, seeking to swell his troop. These
alone were ready to step between the oppressor and
the oppressed. Surely, they were the very best men
you could select to be hung. That was the greatest
compliment which this country could pay them. They
were ripe for her gallows. She has tried a long time,
she has hung a good many, but never found the
right one before.

When I think of him, and his six sons, and his
son in law,—not to enumerate the others,—enlisted for
this fight; proceeding coolly, reverently, humanely to
work, for months if not years, sleeping and waking
upon it, summering and wintering the thought, without expecting any reward but a good conscience,
while almost all America stood ranked on the other
side, I say again that it affects me as a sublime spectacle. If he had had any journal advocating *"his
cause,"* any organ as the phrase is, monotonously and
wearisomely playing the same old tune, and then
passing round the hat, it would have been fatal to
his efficiency. If he had acted in any way so as to be
let alone by the government, he might have been
suspected. It was the fact that the tyrant must give
place to him, or he to the tyrant, that distinguished
him from all the reformers of the day that I know.

It was his peculiar doctrine that a man has a perfect right to interfere by force with the slaveholder, in
order to rescue the slave. I agree with him. They who
are continually shocked by slavery have some right to
be shocked by the violent death of the slaveholder,

but no others. Such will be more shocked by his life than by his death. I shall not be forward to think him mistaken in his method who quickest succeeds to liberate the slave. I speak for the slave when I say, that I prefer the philanthropy of Captain Brown to that philanthropy which neither shoots me nor liberates me. At any rate, I do not think it is quite sane for one to spend his whole life in talking or writing about this matter, unless he is continuously inspired, and I have not done so. A man may have other affairs to attend to. I do not wish to kill nor to be killed, but I can foresee circumstances in which both these things would be by me unavoidable. We preserve the so-called "peace" of our community by deeds of petty violence every day. Look at the policeman's billy and hand cuffs! Look at the jail! Look at the gallows! Look at the chaplain of the regiment! We are hoping only to live safely on the outskirts of *this* provisional army. So we defend ourselves and our hen roosts, and maintain slavery. I know that the mass of my countrymen think that the only righteous use that can be made of Sharps' rifles and revolvers is to fight duels with them, when we are insulted by other nations, or to hunt Indians, or shoot fugitive slaves with them, or the like. I think that for once the Sharps' rifles and the revolvers were employed in a righteous cause. The tools were in the hands of one who could use them.

The same indignation that is said to have cleared the temple once will clear it again. The question is not about the weapon, but the spirit in which you use it. No man has appeared in America as yet who loved his fellow man so well, and treated him so tenderly. He lived for him. He took up his life and he laid it down for him. What sort of violence is that which is encouraged, not by soldiers but by peaceable citizens, not so much by lay-men as by ministers of the gospel, not so much by the fighting sects as by the Quakers, and not so much by Quaker men as by Quaker women?

This event advertises me that there is such a fact as death—the possibility of a man's dying. It seems as if no man had ever died in America before, for in order to die you must first have lived. I dont believe in the hearses and palls and funerals that they have had. There was no death in the case, because there had been no life; they merely rotted or sloughed off, pretty much as they had rotted or sloughed along. No temple's vail was rent, only a hole dug somewhere. Let the dead bury their dead. The best of them fairly ran down like a clock. Franklin—Washington—they were let off without dying; they were merely missing one day. I hear a good many pretend that they are going to die;—or that they have died for aught that I know. Nonsense! I'll defy them to do it. They haven't got life enough in them. They'll deliquesce like fungi, and keep a hundred eulogists mopping the spot where they left off. Only half a dozen or so have died since the world began. Do you think that you are going to die, sir? No! there's no hope of you. You haven't got your lesson yet. You've got to stay after school. We make a needless ado about capital punishment—taking lives, when there is no life to take. *Memento mori!* We don't understand that sublime sentence which some worthy got sculptured on his gravestone once. We've interpreted it in a grovelling and snivelling sense; we've wholly forgotten how to die.

But be sure you do die, neverthless. Do your work, and finish it. If you know how to begin, you will know when to end.

These men, in teaching us how to die, have at the same time taught us how to live. If this man's acts and words do not create a revival, it will be the severest possible satire on the acts and words that do. It is the best news that America has ever heard. It has already quickened the feeble pulse of the North, and infused more and more generous blood into her veins and heart, than any number of years of what is called commercial and political prosperity could. How many a man who was lately contemplating suicide has now something to live for!

One writer says that Brown's peculiar monomania made him to be "dreaded by the Missourians as a supernatural being." Sure enough, a hero in the midst of us cowards is always so dreaded. He is just that thing. He shows himself superior to nature. He has a spark of divinity in him.

> "Unless above himself he can
> Erect himself, how poor a thing is man!"

Newspaper editors argue also that it is a proof of his *insanity* that he thought he was appointed to do this work which he did—that he did not suspect himself for a moment! They talk as if it were impossible that a man could be "divinely appointed" in these days to do any work whatever; as if vows and religion were out of date as connected with any man's daily work,—as if the agent to abolish Slavery could only be somebody appointed by the President, or by some political party. They talk as if a man's death were a failure, and his continued life, be it of whatever character, were a success.

When I reflect to what a cause this man devoted himself, and how religiously, and then reflect to what cause his judges and all who condemn him so angrily and fluently devote themselves, I see that they are as far apart as the heavens and earth are asunder.

The amount of it is, our *"leading men"* are a harm-

less kind of folk, and they know *well enough* that
they were not divinely appointed, but elected by the
votes of their party.

Who is it whose safety requires that Captain Brown
be hung? Is it indispensable to any Northern man?
Is there no resource but to cast these men also to
the Minotaur? If you do not wish it say so distinctly.
While these things are being done, beauty stands
veiled and music is a screeching lie. Think of him—
of his rare qualities! such a man as it takes ages to
make, and ages to understand; no mock hero, nor the
representative of any party. A man such as the sun
may not rise upon again in this benighted land. To
whose making went the costliest material, the finest
adamant; sent to be the redeemer of those in captivity. And the only use to which you can put him is to
hang him at the end of a rope! You who pretend to
care for Christ crucified, consider what you are about
to do to him who offered himself to be the savior of
four millions of men.

Any man knows when he is justified, and all the
wits in the world cannot enlighten him on that point.
The murderer always knows that he is justly punished; but when a government takes the life of a man
without the consent of his conscience, it is an auda-
cious government, and is taking a step towards its
own dissolution. Is it not possible that an individual
may be right and a government wrong? Are laws to
be enforced simply because they were made? or declared by any number of men to be good, if they are
not good? Is there any necessity for a man's being a
tool to perform a deed of which his better nature dis-
approves? Is it the intention of law-makers that *good*
men shall be hung ever? Are judges to interpret the law
according to the letter, and not the spirit? What right
have *you* to enter into a compact with yourself that

you *will* do thus or so, against the light within you? Is it for *you* to *make up* your mind—to form any resolution whatever—and not accept the convictions that are forced upon you, and which ever pass your understanding? I do not believe in lawyers, in that mode of attacking or defending a man, because you descend to meet the judge on his own ground, and, in cases of the highest importance, it is of no consequence whether a man breaks a human law or not. Let lawyers decide trivial cases. Business men may arrange that among themselves. If they were the interpreters of the everlasting laws which rightfully bind man, that would be another thing. A counterfeiting law-factory, standing half in a slave land and half in a free! What kind of laws for free men can you expect from that?

I am here to plead his cause with you. I plead not for his life, but for his character—his immortal life; and so it becomes your cause wholly, and is not his in the least. Some eighteen hundred years ago Christ was crucified; this morning, perchance, Captain Brown was hung. These are the two ends of a chain which is not without its links. He is not Old Brown any longer; he is an Angel of Light.

I see now that it was necessary that the bravest and humanest man in all the country should be hung. Perhaps he saw it himself. I *almost fear* that I may yet hear of his deliverance, doubting if a prolonged life, if *any* life, can do as much good as his death.

"Misguided"! "Garrulous"! "Insane"! "Vindictive"! So ye write in your easy chairs, and thus he wounded responds from the floor of the Armory, clear as a cloudless sky, true as the voice of nature is: "No man sent me here; it was my own prompting and that of my Maker. I acknowledge no master in human form."

And in what a sweet and noble strain he proceeds, addressing his captors, who stand over him: "I think, my friends, you are guilty of a great wrong against God and humanity, and it would be perfectly right for any one to interfere with you so far as to free those you wilfully and wickedly hold in bondage."

And referring to his movement: "It is, in my opinion, the greatest service a man can render to God."

"I pity the poor in bondage that have none to help them; that is why I am here; not to gratify any personal animosity, revenge, or vindictive spirit. It is my sympathy with the oppressed and the wronged, that are as good as you, and as precious in the sight of God."

You don't know your testament when you see it.

"I want you to understand that I respect the rights of the poorest and weakest of colored people, oppressed by the slave power, just as much as I do those of the most wealthy and powerful."

"I wish to say, furthermore, that you had better, all you people at the South, prepare yourselves for a settlement of that question, that must come up for settlement sooner than you are prepared for it. The sooner you are prepared the better. You may dispose of me very easily. I am nearly disposed of now; but this question is still to be settled—this negro question, I mean; the end of that is not yet."

I foresee the time when the painter will paint that scene, no longer going to Rome for a subject; the poet will sing it; the historian record it; and, with the Landing of the Pilgrims and the Declaration of Independence, it will be the ornament of some future national gallery, when at least the present form of Slavery shall be no more here. We shall then be at liberty to weep for Captain Brown. Then, and not till then, we will take our revenge.

Martyrdom of John Brown

So universal and widely related is any transcendent moral greatness—so nearly identical with greatness every where and in every age, as a pyramid contracts the nearer you approach its apex—that, when I now look over my commonplace book of poetry, I find that the best of it is oftenest applicable, in part or wholly, to the case of Captain Brown. Only what is true, and strong, and solemnly earnest will recommend itself to our mood at this time. Almost any noble verse may be read, either as his elegy, or eulogy, or be made the text of an oration on him. Indeed, such are now discerned to be the parts of a universal liturgy, applicable to those rare cases of heroes and martyrs, for which the ritual of no church has provided. This is the formula established on high, —their burial service—to which every great genius has contributed its stanza or line. As Marvell wrote,

> "When the sword glitters o'er the judge's head,
> And fear has coward churchmen silenced,
> Then is the poet's time; 'tis then he draws,
> And single fights forsaken virtue's cause.
> He when the wheel of empire whirleth back,
> And though the world's disjointed axel crack,
> Sings still of ancient rights and better times,
> Seeks suff'ring good, arraigns successful crimes."

The sense of grand poetry, read by the light of this event, is brought out distinctly, like an invisible writing held to the fire.

> "All heads must come
> To the cold tomb,
> Only the actions of the just
> Smell sweet and blossom in the dust."

We have heard that the Boston lady who recently visited our hero in prison found him wearing still the clothes all cut and torn by sabres and by bayonet thrusts, in which he had been taken prisoner; and thus he had gone to his trial, and without a hat. She spent her time in the prison mending those clothes, and, for a memento, brought home a pin covered with blood.—What are the clothes that endure?

> "The garments lasting evermore
> Are works of mercy to the poor;
> And neither tetter, time, nor moth
> Shall fray that silk, or fret this cloth."

The well known verses called "The Soul's Errand," supposed, by some, to have been written by Sir Walter Raleigh, when he was expecting to be executed the following day, are at least worthy of such an origin, and are equally applicable to the present case. Hear them.

> Go, Soul, the body's guest,
>   Upon a thankless arrant;
> Fear not to touch the best,
>   The truth shall be thy warrant:
>   Go, since I needs must die,
>   And give the world the lie.
>
> Go, tell the court it glows
>   And shines like rotten wood;
> Go, tell the church it shows
>   What's good, and doth no good;
>   If church and court reply,
>   Then give them both the lie.
>
> Tell potentates they live
>   Acting by others' actions;
> Not loved unless they give,
>   Not strong but by their factions:
>   If potentates reply,
>   Give potentates the lie.

Tell men of high condition,
   That rule affairs of state,
Their purpose is ambition,
   Their practice only hate;
     And if they once reply,
     Then give them all the lie.

Tell zeal, it lacks devotion;
   Tell love, it is but lust;
Tell time, it is but motion;
   Tell flesh, it is but dust;
     And wish them not reply,
     For thou must give the lie.

Tell age, it daily wasteth;
   Tell honor, how it alters;
Tell beauty, how she blasteth;
   Tell favor, how she falters;
     And as they shall reply,
     Give each of them the lie.

Tell fortune of her blindness;
   Tell nature of decay;
Tell friendship of unkindness;
   Tell justice of delay;
     And if they dare reply,
     Then give them all the lie.

And when thou hast, as I
   Commanded thee, done blabbing,
Although to give the lie
   Deserves no less than stabbing,
     Yet stab at thee who will,
     No stab the soul can kill.

   "When I am dead,
     Let not the day be writ—"
   *Nor bell be tolled—**
     "Love will remember it"
   When hate is cold.

* The selectmen of the town refused to allow the bell to be tolled on this occasion.

You, Agricola, are fortunate, not only because your life was glorious, but because your death was timely. As they tell us who heard your last words, unchanged and willing you accepted your fate; as if, as far as in your power, you would make the emperor appear innocent. But, besides the bitterness of having lost a parent, it adds to our grief, that it was not permitted us to minister to your health, . . . to gaze on your countenance, and receive your last embrace; surely, we might have caught some words and commands which we could have treasured in the inmost part of our souls. This is our pain, this our wound. . . . You were buried with the fewer tears, and in your last earthly light, your eyes looked around for something which they did not see.

If there is any abode for the spirits of the pious; if, as wise men suppose, great souls are not extinguished with the body, may you rest placidly, and call your family from weak regrets, and womanly laments, to the contemplation of your virtues, which must not be lamented, either silently or aloud. Let us honor you by our admiration, rather than by short-lived praises, and, if nature aid us, by our emulation of you. That is true honor, that the piety of whoever is most akin to you. This also I would teach your family, so to venerate your memory, as to call to mind all your actions and words, and embrace your character and the form of your soul, rather than of your body; not because I think that statues which are made of marble or brass are to be condemned, but as the features of men, so images of the features, are frail and perishable. The form of the soul is eternal; and this we can retain and express, not by a foreign material and art, but by our own lives. Whatever of Agricola we have loved, whatever we have admired, remains, and will remain, in the minds of men, and the records of history, through the eternity of ages. For oblivion will overtake many of the ancients, as if they were inglorious and ignoble: Agricola, described and transmitted to posterity, will survive.[1]

[1] Translated by Thoreau from Tacitus [editor's note].

The Last Days of John Brown

JOHN Brown's career for the last six weeks of his life was meteor-like, flashing through the darkness in which we live. I know of nothing so miraculous in our history.

If any person, in a lecture or conversation at that time, cited any ancient example of heroism, such as Cato or Tell or Winkelried, passing over the recent deeds and words of Brown, it was felt by any intelligent audience of Northern men to be tame and inexcusably far-fetched.

For my own part, I commonly attend more to nature than to man, but any affecting human event may blind our eyes to natural objects. I was so absorbed in him as to be surprised whenever I detected the routine of the natural world surviving still, or met persons going about their affairs indifferent. It appeared strange to me that the 'little dipper' should be still diving quietly in the river, as of yore; and it suggested that this bird might continue to dive here when Concord should be no more.

I felt that he, a prisoner in the midst of his enemies, and under sentence of death, if consulted as to his next step or resource, could answer more wisely than all his countrymen beside. He best understood his position; he contemplated it most calmly. Comparatively, all other men, North and South, were beside themselves. Our thoughts could not revert to any greater or wiser or better man with whom to contrast him, for he, then and there, was above them all. The man this country was about to hang appeared the greatest and best in it.

Years were not required for a revolution of public opinion; days, nay, hours, produced marked changes in this case. Fifty who were ready to say on going into our meeting in honor of him in Concord, that he ought to be hung, would not say it when they came out. They heard his words read, they saw the earnest faces of the congregation; and perhaps they joined at last in singing the hymn in his praise.

The order of instructors was reversed. I heard that one preacher, who at first was shocked and stood aloof, felt obliged at last, after he was hung, to make him the subject of a sermon, in which, to some extent, he eulogized the man, but said that his act was a failure. An influential class-teacher thought it necessary, after the services, to tell his grown-up pupils, that at first he thought as the preacher did then, but now he thought that John Brown was right. But it was understood that his pupils were as much ahead of the teacher, as he was ahead of the priest; and I know for a certainty, that very little boys at home had already asked their parents, in a tone of surprise, why God did not interfere to save him. In each case, the constituted teachers were only half conscious that they were not *leading*, but being *dragged*, with some loss of time and power.

The more conscientious preachers, the Bible men, they who talk about principle, and doing to others as you would that they should do unto you,—how could they fail to recognize him, by far the greatest preacher of them all, with the Bible in his life and in his acts, the embodiment of principle, who actually carried out the golden rule? All whose moral sense had been aroused, who had a calling from on high to preach, sided with him. What confessions he extracted from the cold and conservative! It is remarkable, but on the whole it is well, that it did not prove the occasion for a new sect of *Brownites* being formed in our midst.

They, whether within the Church or out of it, who adhere to the spirit and let go the letter, and are accordingly called infidel, were as usual foremost to recognize him. Men have been hung in the South before for attempting to rescue slaves, and the North was not much stirred by it. Whence, then, this wonderful difference? We were not so sure of *their* devotion to principle. We made a subtle distinction, forgot human laws, and did homage to an idea. The North, I mean the *living* North, was suddenly all transcendental. It went behind the human law, it went behind the apparent failure, and recognized eternal justice and glory. Commonly, men live according to a formula, and are satisfied if the order of law is observed, but in this instance they, to some extent, returned to original perceptions, and there was a slight revival of old religion. They saw that what was called order was confusion, what was called justice, injustice, and that the best was deemed the worst. This attitude suggested a more intelligent and generous spirit than that which actuated our forefathers, and the possibility, in the course of ages, of a revolution in behalf of another and an oppressed people.

Most Northern men, and a few Southern ones, were wonderfully stirred by Brown's behavior and words. They saw and felt that they were heroic and noble, and that there had been nothing quite equal to them in their kind in this country, or in the recent history of the world. But the minority were unmoved by them. They were only surprised and provoked by the attitude of their neighbors. They saw that Brown was Brave, and that he believed that he had done right, but they did not detect any further peculiarity in him. Not being accustomed to make fine distinctions, or to appreciate magnanimity, they read his letters and speeches as if they read them not. They were not aware when they approached a heroic statement —they did not know when they *burned*. They did not feel that he spoke with authority, and hence they only remembered that the *law* must be executed. They remembered the old formula, but did not hear the new revelation. The man who does not recognize in Brown's words a wisdom and nobleness, and therefore an authority, superior to our laws, is a modern Democrat. This is the test by which to discover him. He is not wilfully but constitutionally blind on this side, and he is consistent with himself. Such has been his past life; no doubt of it. In like manner he has read history and his Bible, and he accepts, or seems to accept, the last only as an established formula, and not because he has been convicted by it. You will not find kindred sentiments in his common-place book, if he has one.

When a noble deed is done, who is likely to appreciate it? They who are noble themselves. I was not surprised that certain of my neighbors spoke of John Brown as an ordinary felon, for who are they? They have either much flesh, or much office, or much coarseness of some kind. They are not etherial natures in any sense. The dark qualities predominate in them. Several of them are decidedly pachydermatous. I say it in sorrow, not in anger. How can a man behold the light, who has no answering inward light? They are true to their *right*, but when they look this way they *see* nothing, they are blind. For the children of the light to contend with them is as if there should be a contest between eagles and owls. Show me a man who feels bitterly toward John Brown, and let me hear what noble verse he can repeat. He'll be as dumb as if his lips were stone.

It is not every man who can be a Christian, even in a very moderate sense, whatever education you give him. It is a matter of constitution and temperament, after all. He may have to be born again many times. I have known many a man who pretended to be a Christian, in whom it was ridiculous, for he had no genius for it. It is not every man who can be a freeman, even.

Editors persevered for a good while in saying that Brown was crazy: but at last they said only that it was 'a crazy scheme,' and the only evidence brought to prove it was that it cost him his life. I have no doubt that if he had gone with five thousand men, liberated a thousand slaves, killed a hundred or two slaveholders, and had as many more killed on his own side, but not lost his own life, these same editors would have called it by a more respectable name. Yet he has been far more successful than that. He has liberated many thousands of slaves, both North and South. They seem to have known nothing about living or dying for a principle. They all called him crazy then; who calls him crazy now?

All through the excitement occasioned by his remarkable attempt and subsequent behavior, the Massachusetts Legislature, not taking any steps for the defence of her citizens who were likely to be carried to Virginia as witnesses and exposed to the violence of a slaveholding mob, was wholly absorbed in a liquor-agency question, and indulging in poor jokes on the word 'extension.' Bad spirits occupied their thoughts. I am sure that no statesman up to the occasion could have attended to that question at all at that time,—a very vulgar question to attend to at any time.

When I looked into a liturgy of the Church of England, printed near the end of the last century, in order to find a service applicable to the case of Brown, I found that the only martyr recognized and provided

for by it was King Charles the First, an eminent
scamp. Of all the inhabitants of England and of the
world, he was the only one according to this authority, whom that church had made a martyr and saint
of; and for more than a century it had celebrated his
martyrdom, so called, by an annual service. What a
satire on the Church is that!

Look not to legislatures and churches for your
guidance, nor to any soulless, *incorporated* bodies,
but to *inspirited* or inspired ones.

What avail all your scholarly accomplishments
and learning, compared with wisdom and manhood?
To omit his other behavior, see what a work this comparatively unread and unlettered man wrote within
six weeks. Where is our professor of *belles lettres* or
of logic and rhetoric, who can write so well? He wrote
in prison, not a history of the world, like Raleigh,
but an American book which I think will live longer
than that. I do not know of such words, uttered under
such circumstances, and so copiously withal, in Roman or English or any history. What a variety of
themes he touched on in that short space! There are
words in that letter to his wife, respecting the education of his daughters, which deserve to be framed
and hung over every mantlepiece in the land. Compare this earnest wisdom with that of Poor Richard.

The death of Irving, which at any other time would
have attracted universal attention, having occurred
while these things were transpiring, went almost un-
observed. I shall have to read of it in the biography
of authors.

Literary gentlemen, editors and critics, think that
they know how to write, because they have studied
grammar and rhetoric; but they are egregiously mistaken. The *art* of composition is as simple as the dis-

charge of a bullet from a rifle, and its master-pieces imply an infinitely greater force behind them. This unlettered man's speaking and writing are standard English. Some words and phrases deemed vulgarisms and Americanisms before, he has made standard American; such as 'It *will pay.*' It suggests that the one great rule of composition—and if I were a professor of rhetoric, I should insist on this—is to *speak the truth.* This first, this second, this third; pebbles in your mouth or not. This demands earnestness and manhood chiefly.

We seem to have forgotten that the expression, a *liberal* education, originally meant among the Romans one worthy of *free* men; while the learning of trades and professions by which to get your livelihood merely, was considered worthy of *slaves* only. But taking a hint from the word, I would go a step further and say, that it is not the man of wealth and leisure simply, though devoted to art, or science, or literature, who, in a true sense, is *liberally* educated, but only the earnest and *free* man. In a slaveholding country like this, there can be no such thing as a *liberal* education tolerated by the State; and those scholars of Austria and France who, however learned they may be, are contented under their tyrannies, have received only a *servile* education.

Nothing could his enemies do, but it redounded to his infinite advantage—that is, to the advantage of his cause. They did not hang him at once, but reserved him to preach to them. And then there was another great blunder. They did not hang his four followers with him; that scene was still postponed; and so his victory was prolonged and completed. No theatrical manager could have arranged things so wisely to give effect to his behavior and words. And who, think you, *was* the manager? Who placed the slave woman and her child, whom he stooped to kiss for a symbol, between his prison and the gallows?

We soon saw, as he saw, that he was not to be pardoned or rescued by men. That would have been to disarm him, to restore to him a material weapon, a Sharps' rifle, when he had taken up the sword of the spirit—the sword with which he has really won his greatest and most memorable victories. Now he has not laid aside the sword of the spirit, for he is pure spirit himself, and his sword is pure spirit also.

> 'He nothing common did or mean
> Upon that memorable scene,
> Nor called the gods with vulgar spite,
> To vindicate his helpless right;
> But bowed his comely head
> Down as upon a bed.'

What a transit was that of his horizontal body alone, but just cut down from the gallows-tree! We read, that at such a time it passed through Philadelphia, and by Saturday night had reached New York. Thus, like a meteor it shot through the Union from the southern regions toward the north! No such freight had the cars borne since they carried him southward alive.

On the day of his translation, I heard, to be sure, that he was *hung*, but I did not know what that meant; I felt no sorrow on that account; but not for a day or two did I even *hear* that he was *dead*, and not after any number of days shall I believe it. Of all the men who were said to be my contemporaries, it seemed to me that John Brown was the only one who *had not died*. I never hear of a man named Brown now,—and I hear of them pretty often,—I never hear of any particularly brave and earnest man, but my first thought is of John Brown, and what relation he may be to him. I meet him at every turn. He is more alive than ever he was. He has earned immortality. He is not confined to North Elba nor to Kansas. He is no longer working in secret. He works in public, and in the clearest light that shines on this land.

Life without Principle

AT a lyceum, not long since, I felt that the lecturer had chosen a theme too foreign to himself, and so failed to interest me as much as he might have done. He described things not in or near to his heart, but toward his extremities and superficies. There was, in this sense, no truly central or centralizing thought in the lecture. I would have had him deal with his privatest experience, as the poet does. The greatest compliment that was ever paid me was when one asked me what I *thought*, and attended to my answer. I am surprised, as well as delighted, when this happens, it is such a rare use he would make of me, as if he were acquainted with the tool. Commonly, if men want anything of me, it is only to know how many acres I make of their land,—since I am a surveyor,—or, at most, what trivial news I have burdened myself with. They never will go to law for my meat; they prefer the shell. A man once came a considerable distance to ask me to lecture on Slavery; but on conversing with him, I found that he and his clique expected seven-eighths of the lecture to be theirs, and only one-eighth mine; so I declined. I take it for granted, when I am invited to lecture anywhere,—for I have had a little experience in that business,—that there is a desire to hear what I *think* on some subject, though I may be the greatest fool in the country,—and not that I should say pleasant things merely, or such as the audience will assent to; and I resolve, accordingly, that I will give them a strong dose of myself. They have sent for me, and engaged to pay for me, and I am determined that they shall have me, though I bore them beyond all precedent.

So now I would say something similar to you, my

readers. Since *you* are my readers, and I have not been much of a traveller, I will not talk about people a thousand miles off, but come as near home as I can. As the time is short, I will leave out all the flattery, and retain all the criticism.

Let us consider the way in which we spend our lives.

This world is a place of business. What an infinite bustle! I am awaked almost every night by the panting of the locomotive. It interrupts my dreams. There is no sabbath. It would be glorious to see mankind at leisure for once. It is nothing but work, work, work. I cannot easily buy a blank-book to write thoughts in; they are commonly ruled for dollars and cents. An Irishman, seeing me making a minute in the fields, took it for granted that I was calculating my wages. If a man was tossed out of a window when an infant, and so made a cripple for life, or scared out of his wits by the Indians, it is regretted chiefly because he was thus incapacitated for—business! I think that there is nothing, not even crime, more opposed to poetry, to philosophy, ay, to life itself, than this incessant business.

There is a coarse and boisterous money-making fellow in the outskirts of our town, who is going to build a bank-wall under the hill along the edge of his meadow. The powers have put this into his head to keep him out of mischief, and he wishes me to spend three weeks digging there with him. The result will be that he will perhaps get some more money to hoard, and leave for his heirs to spend foolishly. If I do this, most will commend me as an industrious and hardworking man; but if I choose to devote myself to certain labors which yield more real profit, though but little money, they may be inclined to look on me as an idler. Nevertheless, as I do not need the police of

meaningless labor to regulate me, and do not see anything absolutely praiseworthy in this fellow's under-
taking, any more than in many an enterprise of our
own or foreign governments, however amusing it may
be to him or them, I prefer to finish my education at
a different school.

If a man walk in the woods for love of them half
of each day, he is in danger of being regarded as a
loafer; but if he spends his whole day as a speculator, shearing off those woods and making earth
bald before her time, he is esteemed an industrious
and enterprising citizen. As if a town had no interest
in its forests but to cut them down!

Most men would feel insulted, if it were proposed
to employ them in throwing stones over a wall, and
then in throwing them back, merely that they might
earn their wages. But many are no more worthily
employed now. For instance: just after sunrise, one
summer morning, I noticed one of my neighbors walking beside his team, which was slowly drawing a
heavy hewn stone swung under the axle, surrounded
by an atmosphere of industry,—his day's work begun,
—his brow commenced to sweat,—a reproach to all
sluggards and idlers,—pausing abreast the shoulders
of his oxen, and half turning round with a flourish of
his merciful whip, while they gained their length on
him. And I thought, Such is the labor which the
American Congress exists to protect,—honest, manly
toil,—honest as the day is long,—that makes his bread
taste sweet, and keeps society sweet,—which all men
respect and have consecrated: one of the sacred band,
doing the needful, but irksome drudgery. Indeed, I felt
a slight reproach, because I observed this from the
window, and was not abroad and stirring about a
similar business. The day went by, and at evening I
passed the yard of another neighbor, who keeps many

servants, and spends much money foolishly, while he
adds nothing to the common stock, and there I saw
the stone of the morning lying beside a whimsical
structure intended to adorn this Lord Timothy Dex-
ter's premises, and the dignity forthwith departed
from the teamster's labor, in my eyes. In my opinion,
the sun was made to light worthier toil than this. I
may add, that his employer has since run off, in debt
to a good part of the town, and, after passing through
Chancery, has settled somewhere else, there to become once more a patron of the arts.

The ways by which you may get money almost
without exception lead downward. To have done anything by which you earned money *merely* is to have
been truly idle or worse. If the laborer gets no more
than the wages which his employer pays him, he is
cheated, he cheats himself. If you would get money
as a writer or lecturer, you must be popular, which is
to go down perpendicularly. Those services which the
community will most readily pay for it is most dis-
agreeable to render. You are paid for being something
less than a man. The State does not commonly reward a genius any more wisely. Even the poet-laure-
ate would rather not have to celebrate the accidents
of royalty. He must be bribed with a pipe of wine;
and perhaps another poet is called away from his
muse to gauge that very pipe. As for my own business, even that kind of surveying which I could do
with most satisfaction my employers do not want.
They would prefer that I should do my work coarsely
and not too well, ay, not well enough. When I observe
that there are different ways of surveying, my employer commonly asks which will give him the most
land, not which is most correct. I once invented a
rule for measuring cord-wood, and tried to introduce
it in Boston; but the measurer there told me that the

sellers did not wish to have their wood measured correctly,—that he was already too accurate for them, and therefore they commonly got their wood measured in Charlestown before crossing the bridge.

The aim of the laborer should be, not to get his living, to get "a good job," but to perform well a certain work; and, even in a pecuniary sense, it would be economy for a town to pay its laborers so well that they would not feel that they were working for low ends, as for a livelihood merely, but for scientific, or even moral ends. Do not hire a man who does your work for money, but him who does it for love of it.

It is remarkable that there are few men so well employed, so much to their minds, but that a little money or fame would commonly buy them off from their present pursuit. I see advertisements for *active* young men, as if activity were the whole of a young man's capital. Yet I have been surprised when one has with confidence proposed to me, a grown man, to embark in some enterprise of his, as if I had absolutely nothing to do, my life having been a complete failure hitherto. What a doubtful compliment this is to pay me! As if he had met me half-way across the ocean beating up against the wind, but bound nowhere, and proposed to me to go along with him! If I did, what do you think the underwriters would say? No, no! I am not without employment at this stage of the voyage. To tell the truth, I saw an advertisement for able-bodied seamen, when I was a boy, sauntering in my native port, and as soon as I came of age I embarked.

The community has no bribe that will tempt a wise man. You may raise money enough to tunnel a mountain, but you cannot raise money enough to hire a man who is minding *his own* business. An efficient and valuable man does what he can, whether the community pay him for it or not. The inefficient offer their inefficiency to the highest bidder, and are forever expecting to be put into office. One would suppose that they were rarely disappointed.

Perhaps I am more than usually jealous with respect to my freedom. I feel that my connection with and obligation to society are still very slight and transient. Those slight labors which afford me a livelihood, and by which it is allowed that I am to some extent serviceable to my contemporaries, are as yet commonly a pleasure to me, and I am not often reminded that they are a necessity. So far I am successful. But I foresee, that, if my wants should be much increased, the labor required to supply them would become a drudgery. If I should sell both my forenoons and afternoons to society, as most appear to do, I am sure, that, for me, there would be nothing left worth living for. I trust that I shall never thus sell my birthright for a mess of pottage. I wish to suggest that a man may be very industrious, and yet not spend his time well. There is no more fatal blunderer than he who consumes the greater part of his life getting his living. All great enterprises are self-supporting. The poet, for instance, must sustain his body by his poetry, as a steam planing-mill feeds its boilers with the shavings it makes. You must get your living by loving. But as it is said of the merchants that ninety-seven in a hundred fail, so the life of men generally, tried by this standard, is a failure, and bankruptcy may be surely prophesied.

Merely to come into the world the heir of a fortune is not to be born, but to be still-born, rather. To be supported by the charity of friends, or a government-pension,—provided you continue to breathe,—by whatever fine synonymes you describe these relations, is to go into the almshouse. On Sundays the poor debtor goes to church to take an account of stock, and finds, of course, that his outgoes have been greater than his income. In the Catholic Church, especially, they go into Chancery, make a clean confession, give up all, and think to start again. Thus men will lie on their backs, talking about the fall of man, and never make an effort to get up.

As for the comparative demand which men make on life, it is an important difference between two, that the one is satisfied with a level success, that his marks can all be hit by point-blank shots, but the other, however low and unsuccessful his life may be, constantly elevates his aim, though at a very slight angle to the horizon. I should much rather be the last man, —though, as the Orientals say, "Greatness doth not approach him who is forever looking down; and all those who are looking high are growing poor."

It is remarkable that there is little or nothing to be remembered written on the subject of getting a living: how to make getting a living not merely honest and honorable, but altogether inviting and glorious; for if *getting* a living is not so, then living is not. One would think, from looking at literature, that this question had never disturbed a solitary individual's musings. Is it that men are too much disgusted with their experience to speak of it? The lesson of value which money teaches, which the Author of the Universe has taken so much pains to teach us, we are inclined to skip altogether. As for the means of living, it is wonderful how indifferent men of all classes are about it, even reformers, so called,—whether they inherit, or earn, or steal it. I think that society has done nothing for us in this respect, or at least has undone what she has done. Cold and hunger seem more friendly to my nature than those methods which men have adopted and advise to ward them off.

The title *wise* is, for the most part, falsely applied. How can one be a wise man, if he does not know any better how to live than other men?—if he is only more cunning and intellectually subtle? Does Wisdom work in a tread-mill? or does she teach how to succeed *by her example*? Is there any such thing as wisdom not applied to life? Is she merely the miller who grinds the finest logic? It is pertinent to ask if Plato got his *living* in a better way or more successfully than his contemporaries,—or did he succumb to the difficulties of life like other men? Did he seem to prevail over some of them merely by indifference, or by assuming grand airs? or find it easier to live, because his aunt remembered him in her will? The ways in which most men get their living, that is, live, are mere make-shifts, and a shirking of the real business of life,—chiefly because they do not know, but partly because they do not mean, any better.

The rush to California, for instance, and the attitude, not merely of merchants, but of philosophers and prophets, so called, in relation to it, reflect the greatest disgrace on mankind. That so many are ready to live by luck, and so get the means of commanding the labor of others less lucky, without contributing any value to society! And that is called enterprise! I know of no more startling development of the immorality of trade, and all the common modes of getting a living. The philosophy and poetry and religion of such a mankind are not worth the dust of a puff-ball. The hog that gets his living by rooting, stirring up the soil so, would be ashamed of such company. If I could command the wealth of all the worlds by lifting my finger, I would not pay *such* a price for it. Even Mahomet knew that God did not make this world in jest. It makes God to be a moneyed gentleman who scatters a handful of pennies in order to see mankind scramble for them. The world's raffle! A subsistence in the domains of Nature a thing to be raffled for! What a comment, what a satire on our institutions! The conclusion will be, that mankind will hang itself upon a tree. And have all the precepts in all the Bibles taught men only this? and is the last and most admirable invention of the human race only an improved muck-rake? Is this the ground on which Orientals and Occidentals meet? Did God direct us so to get our living, digging where we never planted,— and He would, perchance, reward us with lumps of gold?

God gave the righteous man a certificate entitling him to food and raiment, but the unrighteous man found a *facsimile* of the same in God's coffers, and appropriated it, and obtained food and raiment like the former. It is one of the most extensive systems of counterfeiting that the world has seen. I did not know that mankind were suffering for want of gold. I have seen a little of it. I know that it is very malleable, but not so malleable as wit. A grain of gold will gild a great surface, but not so much as a grain of wisdom.

The gold-digger in the ravines of the mountains is as much a gambler as his fellow in the saloons of San Francisco. What difference does it make, whether you shake dirt or shake dice? If you win, society is the loser. The gold-digger is the enemy of the honest laborer, whatever checks and compensations there may be. It is not enough to tell me that you worked hard to get your gold. So does the Devil work hard. The way of transgressors may be hard in many respects. The humblest observer who goes to the mines sees and says that gold-digging is of the character of a lottery; the gold thus obtained is not the same thing with the wages of honest toil. But, practically, he forgets what he has seen, for he has seen only the fact, not the principle, and goes into trade there, that is, buys a ticket in what commonly proves another lottery, where the fact is not so obvious.

After reading Howitt's account of the Australian gold-diggings one evening, I had in my mind's eye, all night, the numerous valleys, with their streams, all cut up with foul pits, from ten to one hundred feet deep, and half a dozen feet across, as close as they can be dug, and partly filled with water,—the locality to which men furiously rush to probe for their fortunes,—uncertain where they shall break ground,—not knowing but the gold is under their camp itself,—sometimes digging one hundred and sixty feet before they strike the vein, or then missing it by a foot,—turned into demons, and regardless of each other's rights, in their thirst for riches,—whole valleys, for thirty miles, suddenly honey-combed by the pits of the miners, so that even hundreds are drowned in them,—standing in water, and covered with mud and clay, they work night and day, dying of exposure and disease. Having read this, and partly forgotten it, I was thinking, accidentally, of my own unsatisfactory life, doing as others do; and with that vision of the diggings still before me, I asked myself, why I might not be washing some gold daily, though it were only the finest particles,—why I might not sink a shaft down to the gold within me, and work that mine. *There* is a Ballarat, a Bendigo for you,—what though it were a Sulky Gully? At any rate, I might pursue some path, however solitary and narrow and crooked, in which I could walk with love and reverence. Whereever a man separates from the multitude, and goes his own way in this mood, there indeed is a fork in the road, though ordinary travellers may see only a gap in the paling. His solitary path across-lots will turn out the *higher way* of the two.

Men rush to California and Australia as if the true gold were to be found in that direction; but that is to go to the very opposite extreme to where it lies. They go prospecting farther and farther away from the true lead, and are most unfortunate when they think themselves most successful. Is not our *native* soil auriferous? Does not a stream from the golden mountains flow through our native valley? and has not this for more than geologic ages been bringing down the shining particles and forming the nuggets for us? Yet, strange to tell, if a digger steal away, prospecting for this true gold, into the unexplored solitudes around us, there is no danger that any will dog his steps, and endeavor to supplant him. He may claim and undermine the whole valley even, both the cultivated and the uncultivated portions, his whole life long in peace, for no one will ever dispute his claim. They will not mind his cradles or his toms. He is not confined to a claim twelve feet square, as at Ballarat, but may mine anywhere, and wash the whole wide world in his tom.

Howitt says of the man who found the great nugget which weighed twenty-eight pounds, at the Bendigo diggings in Australia:—"He soon began to drink; got a horse and rode all about, generally at full gallop, and when he met people, called out to inquire if they knew who he was, and then kindly informed them that he was 'the bloody wretch that had found the nugget.' At last he rode full speed against a tree, and nearly knocked his brains out." I think, however, there was no danger of that, for he had already knocked his brains out against the nugget. Howitt adds, "He is a hopelessly ruined man." But he is a type of the class. They are all fast men. Hear some of the names of the places where they dig:—"Jackass Flat,"—"Sheep's-Head Gully,"—"Murderer's Bar," etc.

Is there no satire in these names? Let them carry their ill-gotten wealth where they will, I am thinking it will still be "Jackass Flat," if not "Murderer's Bar," where they live.

The last resource of our energy has been the robbing of graveyards on the Isthmus of Darien, an enterprise which appears to be but in its infancy; for, according to late accounts, an act has passed its second reading in the legislature of New Granada, regulating this kind of mining; and a correspondent of the *Tribune* writes:—"In the dry season, when the weather will permit of the country being properly prospected, no doubt other rich '*guacas*' [that is, graveyards] will be found." To emigrants he says:—"Do not come before December; take the Isthmus route in preference to the Boca del Toro one; bring no useless baggage, and do not cumber yourself with a tent; but a good pair of blankets will be necessary; a pick, shovel, and axe of good material will be almost all that is required": advice which might have been taken from the "Burker's Guide." And he concludes with this line in Italics and small capitals: "*If you are doing well at home*, STAY THERE," which may fairly be interpreted to mean, "If you are getting a good living by robbing graveyards at home, stay there."

But why go to California for a text? She is the child of New England, bred at her own school and church.

It is remarkable that among all the preachers there are so few moral teachers. The prophets are employed in excusing the ways of men. Most reverend seniors, the *illuminati* of the age, tell me, with a gracious, reminiscent smile, betwixt an aspiration and a shudder, not to be too tender about these things,—to lump all that, that is, make a lump of gold of it. The highest advice I have heard on these subjects was grovelling. The burden of it was,—It is not worth your while to undertake to reform the world in this particular. Do not ask how your bread is buttered; it will make you sick, if you do,—and the like. A man had better starve at once than lose his innocence in the process of getting his bread. If within the sophisticated man there is not an unsophisticated one, then he is but one of the Devil's angels. As we grow old, we live more coarsely, we relax a little in our disciplines, and, to some extent, cease to obey our finest instincts. But we should be fastidious to the extreme of sanity, disregarding the gibes of those who are more unfortunate than ourselves.

In our science and philosophy, even, there is commonly no true and absolute account of things. The spirit of sect and bigotry has planted its hoof amid the stars. You have only to discuss the problem, whether the stars are inhabited or not, in order to discover it. Why must we daub the heavens as well as the earth? It was an unfortunate discovery that Dr. Kane was a Mason, and that Sir John Franklin was another. But it was a more cruel suggestion that possibly that was the reason why the former went in search of the latter. There is not a popular magazine in this country that would dare to print a child's thought on important subjects without comment. It must be submitted to the D. D.s. I would it were the chickadee-dees.

You come from attending the funeral of mankind to attend to a natural phenomenon. A little thought is sexton to all the world.

I hardly know an *intellectual* man, even, who is so broad and truly liberal that you can think aloud in his society. Most with whom you endeavor to talk soon come to a stand against some institution in which they appear to hold stock,—that is, some particular, not universal, way of viewing things. They will continually thrust their own low roof, with its narrow skylight, between you and the sky, when it is the unobstructed heavens you would view. Get out of the way with your cobwebs, wash your windows, I say! In some lyceums they tell me that they have voted to exclude the subject of religion. But how do I know what their religion is, and when I am near to or far from it? I have walked into such an arena and done my best to make a clean breast of what religion I have experienced, and the audience never suspected what I was about. The lecture was as harmless as moonshine to them. Whereas, if I had read to them the biography of the greatest scamps in history, they might have thought that I had written the lives of the deacons of their church. Ordinarily, the inquiry is, Where did you come from? or, Where are you going? That was a more pertinent question which I overheard one of my auditors put to another once,— "What does he lecture for?" It made me quake in my shoes.

To speak impartially, the best men that I know are not serene, a world in themselves. For the most part, they dwell in forms, and flatter and study effect only more finely than the rest. We select granite for the underpinning of our houses and barns; we build fences of stone; but we do not ourselves rest on an under-pinning of granitic truth, the lowest primitive rock. Our sills are rotten. What stuff is the man made of who is not coexistent in our thought with the purest and subtilest truth? I often accuse my finest acquaint-ances of an immense frivolity; for, while there are manners and compliments we do not meet, we do not teach one another the lessons of honesty and sincerity that the brutes do, or of steadiness and solidity that the rocks do. The fault is commonly mutual, however;

for we do not habitually demand any more of each
other.

That excitement about Kossuth, consider how char-
acteristic, but superficial, it was!—only another kind
of politics or dancing. Men were making speeches to
him all over the country, but each expressed only the
thought, or the want of thought, of the multitude.
No man stood on truth. They were merely banded
together, as usual, one leaning on another, and all
together on nothing; as the Hindoos made the world
rest on an elephant, the elephant on a tortoise, and
the tortoise on a serpent, and had nothing to put
under the serpent. For all fruit of that stir we have
the Kossuth hat.

Just so hollow and ineffectual, for the most part,
is our ordinary conversation. Surface meets surface.
When our life ceases to be inward and private, conversation degenerates into mere gossip. We rarely
meet a man who can tell us any news which he has
not read in a newspaper, or been told by his neighbor; and, for the most part, the only difference between us and our fellow is, that he has seen the
newspaper, or been out to tea, and we have not. In
proportion as our inward life fails, we go more constantly and desperately to the post-office. You may
depend on it, that the poor fellow who walks away
with the greatest number of letters, proud of his
extensive correspondence, has not heard from himself
this long while.

I do not know but it is too much to read one newspaper a week. I have tried it recently, and for so long
it seems to me that I have not dwelt in my native
region. The sun, the clouds, the snow, the trees say
not so much to me. You cannot serve two masters.
It requires more than a day's devotion to know and
to possess the wealth of a day.

We may well be ashamed to tell what things we have read or heard in our day. I do not know why my news should be so trivial,—considering what one's dreams and expectations are, why the developments should be so paltry. The news we hear, for the most part, is not news to our genius. It is the stalest repetition. You are often tempted to ask, why such stress is laid on a particular experience which you have had,—that, after twenty-five years, you should meet Hobbins, Registrar of Deeds, again on the sidewalk. Have you not budged an inch, then? Such is the daily news. Its facts appear to float in the atmosphere, insignificant as the sporules of fungi, and impinge on some neglected *thallus*, or surface of our minds, which affords a basis for them, and hence a parasitic growth. We should wash ourselves clean of such news. Of what consequence, though our planet explode, if there is no character involved in the explosion? In health we have not the least curiosity about such events. We do not live for idle amusement. I would not run round a corner to see the world blow up.

All summer, and far into the autumn, perchance, you unconsciously went by the newspapers and the news, and now you find it was because the morning and the evening were full of news to you. Your walks were full of incidents. You attended, not to the affairs of Europe, but to your own affairs in Massachusetts fields. If you chance to live and move and have your being in that thin stratum in which the events that make the news transpire,—thinner than the paper on which it is printed,—then these things will fill the world for you; but if you soar above or dive below that plane, you cannot remember nor be reminded of them. Really to see the sun rise or go down every day, so to relate ourselves to a universal fact, would

preserve us sane forever. Nations! What are nations?
Tartars, and Huns, and Chinamen! Like insects, they
swarm. The historian strives in vain to make them
memorable. It is for want of a man that there are so
many men. It is individuals that populate the world.
Any man thinking may say with the Spirit of Lodin,—

> "I look down from my height on nations,
> And they become ashes before me;—
> Calm is my dwelling in the clouds;
> Pleasant are the great fields of my rest."

Pray, let us live without being drawn by dogs,
Esquimaux-fashion, tearing over hill and dale, and
biting each other's ears.

Not without a slight shudder at the danger, I
often perceive how near I had come to admitting into
my mind the details of some trivial affair,—the news
of the street; and I am astonished to observe how
willing men are to lumber their minds with such
rubbish,—to permit idle rumors and incidents of the
most insignificant kind to intrude on ground which
should be sacred to thought. Shall the mind be a public arena, where the affairs of the street and the gossip of the tea-table chiefly are discussed? Or shall it
be a quarter of heaven itself,—an hypæthral temple,
consecrated to the service of the gods? I find it so difficult to dispose of the few facts which to me are significant, that I hesitate to burden my attention with
those which are insignificant, which only a divine
mind could illustrate. Such is, for the most part, the
news in newspapers and conversation. It is important
to preserve the mind's chastity in this respect. Think
of admitting the details of a single case of the criminal court into our thoughts, to stalk profanely
through their very *sanctum sanctorum* for an hour,
ay, for many hours! to make a very bar-room of the

mind's inmost apartment, as if for so long the dust of
the street had occupied us,—the very street itself, with
all its travel, its bustle, and filth had passed through
our thoughts' shrine! Would it not be an intellectual
and moral suicide? When I have been compelled to
sit spectator and auditor in a court-room for some
hours, and have seen my neighbors, who were not
compelled, stealing in from time to time, and tiptoe-
ing about with washed hands and faces, it has appeared to my mind's eye, that, when they took off
their hats, their ears suddenly expanded into vast
hoppers for sound, between which even their narrow
heads were crowded. Like the vanes of windmills, they
caught the broad, but shallow stream of sound, which,
after a few titillating gyrations in their coggy brains,
passed out the other side. I wondered if, when they
got home, they were as careful to wash their ears as
before their hands and faces. It has seemed to me, at
such a time, that the auditors and the witnesses, the
jury and the counsel, the judge and the criminal at
the bar,—if I may presume him guilty before he is convicted,—were all equally criminal, and a thunderbolt
might be expected to descend and consume them all
together.

By all kinds of traps and sign-boards, threatening
the extreme penalty of the divine law, exclude such
trespassers from the only ground which can be sacred
to you. It is so hard to forget what it is worse than
useless to remember! If I am to be a thoroughfare, I
prefer that it be of the mountain-brooks, the Par-
nassian streams, and not the town-sewers. There is
inspiration, that gossip which comes to the ear of the
attentive mind from the courts of heaven. There is
the profane and stale revelation of the bar-room and
the police court. The same ear is fitted to receive both
communications. Only the character of the hearer

determines to which it shall be open, and to which closed. I believe that the mind can be permanently profaned by the habit of attending to trivial things, so that all our thoughts shall be tinged with triviality. Our very intellect shall be macadamized, as it were,— its foundation broken into fragments for the wheels of travel to roll over; and if you would know what will make the most durable pavement, surpassing rolled stones, spruce blocks, and asphaltum, you have only to look into some of our minds which have been subjected to this treatment so long.

If we have thus desecrated ourselves,—as who has not?—the remedy will be by wariness and devotion to reconsecrate ourselves, and make once more a fane of the mind. We should treat our minds, that is, our-selves, as innocent and ingenuous children, whose guardians we are, and be careful what objects and what subjects we thrust on their attention. Read not the Times. Read the Eternities. Conventionalities are at length as bad as impurities. Even the facts of sci-ence may dust the mind by their dryness, unless they are in a sense effaced each morning, or rather ren-dered fertile by the dews of fresh and living truth. Knowledge does not come to us by details, but in flashes of light from heaven. Yes, every thought that passes through the mind helps to wear and tear it, and to deepen the ruts, which, as in the streets of Pompeii, evince how much it has been used. How many things there are concerning which we might well deliberate, whether we had better know them,— had better let their peddling-carts be driven, even at the slowest trot or walk, over that bridge of glorious span by which we trust to pass at last from the far-thest brink of time to the nearest shore of eternity! Have we no culture, no refinement,—but skill only to live coarsely and serve the Devil?—to acquire a little worldly wealth, or fame, or liberty, and make a false show with it, as if we were all husk and shell, with no tender and living kernel to us? Shall our institutions be like those chestnut-burs which contain abortive nuts, perfect only to prick the fingers?

America is said to be the arena on which the battle of freedom is to be fought; but surely it cannot be freedom in a merely political sense that is meant. Even if we grant that the American has freed himself from a political tyrant, he is still the slave of an economical and moral tyrant. Now that the republic— the *res-publica*—has been settled, it is time to look after the *res-privata*,—the private state,—to see, as the Roman senate charged its consuls, *"ne quid res-*PRIVATA *detrimenti caperet,"* that the *private* state receive no detriment.

Do we call this the land of the free? What is it to be free from King George and continue the slaves of King Prejudice? What is it to be born free and not to live free? What is the value of any political freedom, but as a means to moral freedom? Is it a freedom to be slaves, or a freedom to be free, of which we boast? We are a nation of politicians, concerned about the outmost defences only of freedom. It is our children's children who may perchance be really free. We tax ourselves unjustly. There is a part of us which is not represented. It is taxation without representation. We quarter troops, we quarter fools and cattle of all sorts upon ourselves. We quarter our gross bodies on our poor souls, till the former eat up all the latter's substance.

With respect to a true culture and manhood, we are essentially provincial still, not metropolitan,—mere Jonathans. We are provincial, because we do not find at home our standards,—because we do not worship truth, but the reflection of truth,—because we are warped and narrowed by an exclusive devotion to trade and commerce and manufactures and agriculture and the like, which are but means, and not the end.

So is the English Parliament provincial. Mere country-bumpkins, they betray themselves, when any more important question arises for them to settle, the Irish question, for instance,—the English question why did I not say? Their natures are subdued to what they work in. Their "good breeding" respects only secondary objects. The finest manners in the world are awkwardness and fatuity, when contrasted with a finer intelligence. They appear but as the fashions of past days,—mere courtliness, knee-buckles and small-clothes, out of date. It is the vice, but not the excellence of manners, that they are continually being deserted by the character; they are cast-off clothes or shells, claiming the respect which belonged to the living creature. You are presented with the shells instead of the meat, and it is no excuse generally, that, in the case of some fishes, the shells are of more worth than the meat. The man who thrusts his manners upon me does as if he were to insist on introducing me to his cabinet of curiosities, when I wished to see himself. It was not in this sense that the poet Decker called Christ "the first true gentleman that ever breathed." I repeat that in this sense the most splendid court in Christendom is provincial, having authority to consult about Transalpine interests only, and not the affairs of Rome. A praetor or proconsul would suffice to settle the questions which absorb the attention of the English Parliament and the American Congress.

Government and legislation! these I thought were respectable professions. We have heard of heaven-born Numas, Lycurguses, and Solons, in the history

of the world, whose *names* at least may stand for
ideal legislators; but think of legislating to *regulate*
the breeding of slaves, or the exportation of tobacco!
What have divine legislators to do with the exportation or the importation of tobacco? what humane
ones with the breeding of slaves? Suppose you were
to submit the question to any son of God,—and has
He no children in the nineteenth century? is it a
family which is extinct?—in what condition would
you get it again? What shall a State like Virginia say
for itself at the last day, in which these have been
the principal, the staple productions? What ground is
there for patriotism in such a State? I derive my facts
from statistical tables which the States themselves
have published.

A commerce that whitens every sea in quest of
nuts and raisins, and makes slaves of its sailors for
this purpose! I saw, the other day, a vessel which had
been wrecked, and many lives lost, and her cargo of
rags, juniper-berries, and bitter almonds were strewn
along the shore. It seemed hardly worth the while to
tempt the dangers of the sea between Leghorn and
New York for the sake of a cargo of juniper-berries
and bitter almonds. America sending to the Old World
for her bitters! Is not the sea-brine, is not shipwreck,
bitter enough to make the cup of life go down here?
Yet such, to a great extent, is our boasted commerce;
and there are those who style themselves statesmen
and philosophers who are so blind as to think that
progress and civilization depend on precisely this
kind of interchange and activity,—the activity of flies
about a molasses-hogshead. Very well, observes one,
if men were oysters. And very well, answer I, if men
were mosquitoes.

Lieutenant Herndon, whom our Government sent
to explore the Amazon, and, it is said, to extend the

area of Slavery, observed that there was wanting there "an industrious and active population, who know what the comforts of life are, and who have artificial wants to draw out the great resources of the country." But what are the "artificial wants" to be encouraged? Not the love of luxuries, like the tobacco and slaves of, I believe, his native Virginia, nor the ice and granite and other material wealth of our native New England; nor are "the great resources of a country" that fertility or barrenness of soil which produces these. The chief want, in every State that I have been into, was a high and earnest purpose in its inhabitants. This alone draws out "the great resources" of Nature, and at last taxes her beyond her resources; for man naturally dies out of her. When we want culture more than potatoes, and illumination more than sugar-plums, then the great resources of a world are taxed and drawn out, and the result, or staple production, is, not slaves, nor operatives, but men,— those rare fruits called heroes, saints, poets, philosophers, and redeemers.

In short, as a snow-drift is formed where there is a lull in the wind, so, one would say, where there is a lull of truth, an institution springs up. But the truth blows right on over it, nevertheless, and at length blows it down.

What is called politics is comparatively something so superficial and inhuman, that, practically, I have never fairly recognized that it concerns me at all. The newspapers, I perceive, devote some of their columns specially to politics or government without charge; and this, one would say, is all that saves it; but, as I love literature, and, to some extent, the truth also, I never read those columns at any rate. I do not wish to blunt my sense of right so much. I have not got to answer for having read a single President's Message,

A strange age of the world this, when empires, king-
doms, and republics come a-begging to a private man's
door, and utter their complaints at his elbow! I cannot
take up a newspaper but I find that some wretched
government or other, hard pushed, and on its last
legs, is interceding with me, the reader, to vote for
it,—more importunate than an Italian beggar; and if
I have a mind to look at its certificate, made, perchance, by some benevolent merchant's clerk, or the
skipper that brought it over, for it cannot speak a
word of English itself, I shall probably read of the
eruption of some Vesuvius, or the overflowing of some
Po, true or forged, which brought it into this condition. I do not hesitate, in such a case, to suggest work,
or the almshouse; or why not keep its castle in silence,
as I do commonly? The poor President, what with
preserving his popularity and doing his duty, is completely bewildered. The newspapers are the ruling
power. Any other government is reduced to a few marines at Fort Independence. If a man neglects to read
the Daily Times, Government will go down on its
knees to him, for this is the only treason in these days.

Those things which now most engage the attention
of men, as politics and the daily routine, are, it is
true, vital functions of human society, but should be
unconsciously performed, like the corresponding functions of the physical body. They are *infra*-human, a
kind of vegetation. I sometimes awake to a half-
consciousness of them going on about me, as a man
may become conscious of some of the processes of
digestion in a morbid state, and so have the dyspepsia,
as it is called. It is as if a thinker submitted himself
to be rasped by the great gizzard of creation. Politics
is, as it were, the gizzard of society, full of grit and
gravel, and the two political parties are its two opposite halves,—sometimes split into quarters, it may be,

which grind on each other. Not only individuals, but States, have thus a confirmed dyspepsia, which expresses itself, you can imagine by what sort of eloquence. Thus our life is not altogether a forgetting, but also, alas! to a great extent, a remembering of that which we should never have been conscious of, certainly not in our waking hours. Why should we not meet, not always as dyspeptics, to tell our bad dreams, but sometimes as *eu*peptics, to congratulate each other on the ever glorious morning? I do not make an exorbitant demand, surely.

Reform and the Reformers

THE Reformers are no doubt the true ancestors of the next generation; the Conservative belongs to a decaying family, and has not learned that he who seeks to save his 'life' shall lose it. Both are sick, but the one is already convalescent. His disease is not organic but acute, and he looks forward to coming springs with hope. He is not sick of any incurable disorder, of plague or consumption; but of tradition and conformity and infidelity; but the other is still taking his bitters and quack medicines patiently, and will grow worse yet. The heads of conservatives have a puny and deficient look, a certain callowness and concavity, as if they were prematurely exposed on one or both sides, or were made to lie or pack together, as when several nuts are formed under the same burr where only one should have been. We wonder to see such a head wear a whole hat. Such as these naturally herd together for mutual protection. They say *We* and *Our*, as if they had never been assured of an individual existence. *Our* Indian policy; *our* coast defences, *our* national character. They are what are called public men, fashionable men, ambitious men, chaplains of the army or navy; men of property, standing and respectability, for the most part, and in all cases created by society. Sometimes even they are embarked in "Great Causes" which have been stranded on the shores of society in a previous age, carrying them through with a kind of reflected and traditionary nobleness, certainly disinterestedness. The Conservative has many virtues which the Reformer has not,— ofttimes a singular and unexpected liberality and courtesy, a decided practicalness and reverence for facts, and with a little less irritability, or more indifference would be the more tolerable companion. He is the steward of society, and in this office at least is faithful and generous. He is a dutiful son but a tyrannical father, and does not foresee that unimaginable epoch when the rising generation will have attained to a level with the risen. Rather he is himself a son all his days, and never arrives at such maturity as to be informed that he and such as he are now mankind and the latest generation, the occupants and proprietors of the globe, but he still feels it to be his chief duty to preserve the law and order and institutions which he finds existing.

It is remarkable how well men train. The teamster rolls out of his cradle into a Tom-and-Jerry—and goes at once to look after his team—to fodder and water his horses, without standing agape at his position. What is the destiny of man, compared with the shipping interests? What does he care for—his creator? does'nt he drive for Squire Make-a-Stir?

The ladies of the land with equal bravery are weavers of toilet cushions and tidies not to betray too green an interest in their fates. Men now take snuff into their noses, but if they had been so advised in season, they would have put it into their ears and eyes. They may gravely deny this, but do not believe them.

In the midst of all this disorder and imperfection in human affairs which he would rather avoid to think of comes the Reformer, the impersonation of disorder and imperfection; to heal and reform them; seeking to discover the divine order and conform to it; and earnestly asking the cooperation of men.

No doubt the evil is great and manifest, and something must certainly be done; and his zeal is in proportion to the urgency of the case,—but I know of few radicals as yet who are radical enough, and have

not got this name ratner by meddling with the exposed roots of innocent institutions than with their
own.

The disease and disorder in society are wont to be
referred to the false relations in which men live one
to another, but strictly speaking there can be no such
thing as a false relation; if the condition of the things
related is true. False relations grow out of false condi-
tions. The inmate of a poorhouse would be more
pauper still on a desolate island, and the convict would
find his prison and prison discipline there.

It is not the worst reason why the reform should be
a private and individual enterprise, that perchance
the evil may be private also. From what southern
plains comes up the voice of wailing,—under what
latitudes reside the heathen to whom we would send
light,—and who is that intemperate and brutal man
whom he would redeem?

. Now, if anything ail a man so that he does not
perform his functions; especially if his digestion is
poor, though he may have considerable nervous
strength left; if he has failed in all his undertakings
hitherto; if he has committed some heinous sin and
partially repents, what does he do? He sets about
reforming the world. Do ye hear it, ye Woloffs, ye
Patagonians, ye Tartars, ye Nez Percés? The world is
going to be reformed, formed once for all. Presto –
Change! Methinks I hear the glad tidings spreading
over the green prairies of the west; over the silent
South American pampas, parched African deserts,
and stretching Siberian versts; through the populous
Indian and Chinese villages, along the Indus, the
Ganges, and Hydaspes.

There is no reformer on the globe, no such philan-
thropic—benevolent and charitable man—now engaged
in any good work anywhere, sorely afflicted by the

sight of misery around him, and animated by the desire to relieve it, who would not instantly and unconsciously sign off from these pure labors, and betake himself to purer, if he had but righted some obscure, and perhaps unrecognized private grievance. Let but the spring come to him, let the morning rise over his couch, and he will forsake his generous companions, without apology or explanation!

The Reformer who comes recommending any institution or system to the adoption of men, must not rely solely on logic and argument, or on eloquence and oratory for his success, but see that he represents one pretty perfect institution in himself, the centre and circumference of all others, an erect man.

I ask of all Reformers, of all who are recommending Temperance—Justice—Charity—Peace, the Family, Community or Associative life, not to give us their theory and wisdom only, for these are no proof, but to carry around with them each a small specimen of his own manufactures, and to despair of ever recommending anything of which a small sample at least cannot be exhibited:—that the Temperance man let me know the savor of Temperance, if it be good, the Just man permit to enjoy the blessings of liberty while with him, the Community man allow me to taste the sweets of the Community life in his society.

I cannot bear to be told to wait for good results, I pine as much for good beginnings. We never come to final results, and it is too late to start from perennial beginnings.

But alas, when we ask the schemer to show us the material of which his structure is to be built. He exhibits only fair looking words, resolute and solid words for the underpinning, convenient and homely words for the body of the edifice, poems and flights of the imagination for the dome and cupola.

Men know very well how to distinguish barren words from those which are cousin to a deed, and the promising or threatening speaker is only rated at his faculty and resolution to do what he says. The phlegmatic audience which sits near the doors know that the speaker does not mean to abolish property or dissolve the family tie, or do without human governments all over the world to-night, but that simply, he has agreed to be the speaker and—they have agreed to be the audience. They may chance to know that the lecturer against the use of money is paid for his lecture, and that is the precept which they hear and believe, and they have a great deal of sympathy with him.

After all the peace lectures and non resistance meetings it was never yet learned from them how any of the speakers would conduct in an emergency, because a very important disputant, one Mr Resistance was not present to offer his arguments.

There are not only books, but lectures and sermons of fiction, whether written or extemporaneous. The modern Reformers are a class of *improvvisánti* more wonderful and amusing than the Italians.

What the prophets even have said is forgotten, and the oracles are decayed, but what heroes and saints have done is still remembered, and posterity will tell it again and again.

We rarely see the Reformer who is fairly launched in his enterprise, bringing about the right state of things with hearty and effective tugs, and not rather preparing and grading the way through the minds of the people. What if the community were to pull altogether says he!—Aye, what if two—what if one even were to work harmoniously and with all his energies! say I. No wonder you plead for my cooperation—I could exert myself considerably. It would be worth the while methinks to have my traces hitched to some good institution.

There certainly can be no greater folly than for men to set about to prove a truth at their leisure who have no other business with it. As if one were to proclaim that he was going a long journey, and because one of his neighbors was inattentive or did not believe it, should put it off. To the man of industry and work it is not quite essential that I should *think* with him. When my neighbor is going to build a house, whether for me or for himself, he does not come to me and reproach or pity me for living in a shed, but he digs the cellar and raises the frame, and makes haste to get the roof done, that he may do the inside-work more comfortably, and he knows very well what assistance he can count upon in these labors.

For the most part by simply agreeing in opinion with the preacher and Reformer I defend myself and get rid of him, for he really asks for no sympathy with deeds,—and this trick it would be well for the irritable Conservative to know and practise.

The great benefactors of their race have been single and singular and not masses of men. Whether in poetry or history it is the same: Minerva – Ceres – Neptune – Prometheus – Socrates – Christ – Luther – Columbus – Arkwright.

There is no objection to action in societies or communities when it is the individual using the society as his instrument, rather than the society using the individual. While one's inspiration is so high and pure as to be necessarily solitary and not to be made a subject of sympathy or congratulation, he may safely use any instrument in his way, whether wood or iron or masses of men. But when the vote of the society rises to a level with his own prayers, and its resolution in the least confirms his own, he may suspect himself, or he may suspect his companions. There have been meetings, religious, political and reformatory, to which men came a hundred miles—though all they had to offer were—some resolutions! What becomes of resolutions that have been offered?

In every society there is or was at least one individual, its founder and leader, who did not belong to it, but who imparted to it whatever life and efficiency it had, and sad indeed is the condition of that society, and it is the condition of most, which is deprived of its head—and soul—for the members can still vote,—and as it were by force of galvanism, a spasmodic action be kept up in the body, and men call it life, and expect virtue and character from senseless nerves and muscles. Such societies, as they prize life, will have recourse to dinners and tea-parties that the members may not utterly fail for want of a belly also.

Consider, after all, how very private and silent an affair it is to lead a life—that we do not consider our duties, or the actions of our life, as in a caucus or convention of men, where the subject has been before the meeting a long time, and many resolutions have been proposed and passed, and now one speaker has the floor and then another, and the subject is fairly under discussion; but the convention where our most private and intimate affairs are discussed is very thinly attended, almost we are not there ourselves, that is the go-to-meeting part of us. It is very still, and few resolutions get passed. Few words are spoken, and the hours are not counted!

Next and nearest to that unfortunate man even whom we would stand by in our philanthropy is the mystery of his life. It is nearer than cold or hunger for they are but the outside of it—it is between him and them, and do what we will, we must leave him alone with that.

The information which the gods vouchsafe to give us is never concerning anything which we wished to know. We are not wise enough to put a question to them. Tell me some truth about society and you will annihilate it. What though we are its ailing members and prisoners. We cannot always be detained by your measures for reform. All that is called hindrance without is but occasion within. The prisoner who is free in spirit, on whose innocent life some rays of light and hope still fall, will not delay to be a reformer of prisons, an inventor of superior prison disciplines, but walks forth free on the path by which those rays penetrated to his cell. Has the Green Mountain boy made no better nor more thrilling discovery than that the church is rotten and the state corrupt? Thank heaven, we have not to choose our calling out of those enterprises which society has to offer. Is he then indeed called, who chooses to what he is called? Obey your calling rather, and it will not be whither your neighbors and kind friends and patrons expect or desire, but be true nevertheless, and choose not, nor go whither they call you. "Thy lot or portion of life, is seeking after thee; therefore be at rest from seeking after it."

From the side to which all eyes are turned, and the hue and cry leads, from the effort which the state abets, and the church prays for, the least profitable result comes, the least performance issues.

We would have some pure product of man's hands, some pure labor, some life got in this old trade of getting a living—some work done which shall not be a mending, a cobbling, a reforming. Show me the mountain boy, the city boy, who never heard of an abuse, who has not *chosen* his calling. It is the delight of the ages, the free labor of man, even the creative and beautiful arts.

Be sure your fate
Doth keep apart its state;
Not linked with any band,
Even the nobles of the land;
In tented fields with cloth of gold
No place doth hold,
But is more chivalrous than they are,
And sigheth for a nobler war;
A finer strain its trumpet sings,
A brighter gleam its armor flings.
The life that I aspire to live
No man proposeth me,
Only the promise of my heart
Wears its emblazonry.

How long shall vice give a home to virtue? One generation abandons the enterprises of another. Many an institution which was thought to be an essential part of the order of society, has, in the true order of events, been left like a stranded vessel on the sand.

When a zealous Reformer would fain discourse to me, I would have him consider first if he has anything to say to me. All simple and necessary speech between men is sweet; but it takes calamity, it takes death or great good fortune commonly to bring them together. We are sages and proud to speak when we are the bearers of great news, even though it be hard; to tell a man of the welfare of his kindred in foreign parts, or even that his house is on fire, is a great good fortune, and seems to relate us to him by a worthier tie.

It is a great blessing to have to do with men, to be called to them as simply as into the field of your occupation. It refreshes and invigorates us. But this happiness is rare. For the most part we can only treat one another to our wit, our good manners and equanimity, and though we have eagles to give we demand of each other only coppers. We pray that our companion will demand of us truth, sincerity, love and noble behavior, for now these virtues lie impossible to us, and we only know them by their names. Only lovers know the value and magnanimity of truth, while traders prize a cheap honesty, and neighbors and acquaintances a cheap civility.

If you have nothing to say let me have your silence, for that is good and fertile. Silence is the ambrosial night in the intercourse of men in which their sincerity is recruited and takes deeper root.—There are such vices as frivolity, garrulity, and verbosity, not to mention prophanity, growing out of the abuse of speech which does not belong wholly to antiquity, and none have imparted a more cheerless aspect to society.

A man must serve another and a better use than any he can consciously render. Every class and order in the universe is the heaven of certain gifts to men. There is a whole class of musk bearing animals, and each flower has its peculiar odor. And all these together go to make the general wholesome and invigorating atmosphere. So each man should take care to emit his fragrance, and after all perform some such office as hemlock boughs, or dried and healing herbs. Though you are a Reformer we want not your reasons, your good roots and foundations—nor your uprightness and benevolence which are your stem and leaves—but we want the flower and fruit of the man—that some fragrance at least as of fresh spring life be wafted over from thee to me. This is consolation and that charity that hides a multitude of sins. Our companion must be a sort of appreciable wealth to us or at least make us sensible of our own riches—in his degree an apostle á Mercury, á Ceres, á Minerva, the bearer of diverse gifts to us. He must bring me the morning light untarnished, and the evening red undimmed. There must be the hilarity of spring in his mirth, the summer's serenity in his joy, the autumnal ripeness in his wisdom, and the repose and abundance of winter in his silence. He should impart his courage and not his despair; his health and ease, and not his disease, and take care that this does not spread by contagion.

It is rare that we are able to impart wealth to our fellows, and do not surround them with our own cast off griefs as an atmosphere, and name it sympathy. If we would indeed reform mankind by truly Indian, botanic, magnetic, or *natural* means, let us strive first to be as simple and well as nature ourselves.

I would say therefore to the anxious speculator and philanthropist—Let us dispel the clouds which hang over our own brows—take up a little life into your pores, endeavor to encourage the flow of sap in your veins, find your soil, strike root and grow—Apollo's waters and God will give the increase. Help to clothe the human field with green. Be green and flourishing plants in God's nursery, and not such complaining bleeding trees as Dante saw in the Infernal Regions.

If your branches wither, send out your fibres into every kingdom of nature for its contribution—lift up your boughs into the heavens for etherial and starry influences, let your roots like those of the willow wander wider, deeper, to some moist and fertile spot in the earth, and make firm your trunk against the elements.

Be fast rooted withal in your native soil of originality and independence, your virgin mould of unexhausted strength and fertility—Nor suffer yourself ever to be transplanted again into the foreign and ungenial regions of tradition and conformity, or the lean and sandy soils of public opinion.

What! to be blown about, a creature of the affections, preaching love and good will and charity, with these tender fibres all bare in a cold world, and not a brother kind enough to throw a spade-full of earth over them! Better try what virtue there is in sand even, and cover your roots with the first exhausted soil you can find.

Who shall tell what blossoms, what fruits, what public and private advantage may push up through this rind we call a man? The traveller may stand by him as a perennial fountain in the desert and slake his thirst forever.

The wind rustling the leaves, the brags of some children have thrilled me more than the lives of the greatest and holiest men. What idle sorrow and stereotyped despair in the saints! What wavering performance in the heroes! Even the prophets and redeemers have rather consoled the fears than satisfied the free demands and hopes of man! We know nowhere recorded a simple and irrepressible satisfaction with the gift of life, a memorable and unbribed praise of God. So long as the Reformers are earnest enough and pleased with their own conceptions, they may entertain me, but when the time comes that their theme is exhausted, and only the sad alternative is left to do the things they have said; and they would rather that I should do them, then they are intolerable companions.

I like the old world and I like the new—winter and summer, hay and grass,—but the death that presumes to give laws to life, and persists in affirming essential disease and disorder to the child who has just begun to bathe his senses and his understanding in the perception of order and beauty—that perseveres in maturing its schemes of life till its last days are come, is not to be compared to anything in nature. The growing man or youth, is a fact which commonly we do not enough allow for in our speculations—but to remember which would be fatal to many a fine theory. Speak for yourself, old man. When we are oppressed by the heat and turmoil of the noon, we should remember that the sun which scorches us with his beams, is gilding the hills of morning and awaking the woodland quires for other men. So too it must not be forgotten, the evening exhibits in the still rear of day a beauty to which the morning and the noon are strangers.

It is hard to make those who have talked much, especially preachers and lecturers, deepen their speech, and give it fresh sincerity and significance. It will be a long time before they understand what you mean. They will wonder if you don't value fluency. But the drains flow. Turn your back, and wait till you hear their words ring solid, and they will have cause to thank you! How infinitely trackless yet passable are we. Is not our own interior white on the chart? Inward is a direction which no traveller has taken. Inward is the bourne which all travellers seek and from which none desire to return. There are the sources of the Nile and Niger.

Every man is the lord of a realm beside which the earthly empire of the Czars is but a petty state—with its ocean borders—its mountain ranges, and its trackless paradises of unfallen nature. And, O ye Reformers! if the good Gods have given ye any high ray of truth to be wrought into life, here in your own realms without let or hindrance is the application to be made.

Those who dwell in Oregon and the far west are not so solitary as the enterprising and independent thinker, applying his discoveries to his own life. This is the way we would see a man striving with his axe and kettle to take up his abode. To this rich soil should the New Englander wend his way. Here is

Wisconsin and the farthest west. It is simple, independent, original, natural life.

Most whom I meet in the streets are, so to speak, outward bound, they live out and out, are going and coming, looking before and behind, all out of doors and in the air. I would fain see them inward bound, retiring in and in, farther and farther every day, and when I inquired for them I should not hear, that they had gone abroad anywhere, to Rondont or Sackets Harbor, but that they had withdrawn deeper within the folds of being.

England and France, Spain and Portugal, Gold Coast and Slave Coast, all front upon this private sea, but no bark from them has ventured out of sight of land,—though it is without a doubt the direct way to India.

I would say then to my vagrant countrymen—Go not to any foreign theater for spectacles, but consider first that there is nothing which can delight or astonish the eyes, but you may discover it all in yourselves. One hastens to Southern Africa perchance to chase the giraffe; but that is not the game he would be after. How long, pray, would a man hunt giraffes, if he could?— What was the meaning of that Exploring Expedition with all its parade and expense, but a recognition of the fact that there are continents and seas in the moral world to which every man is an inlet, yet unexplored by him; but that it is easier to sail many thousand miles through cold and storms and savage cannibals, in a government ship, with 500 men and boys to steer and sail for one, than it is to explore the private sea, the Atlantic and Pacific ocean of one's being alone.

> Erret, et extremos alter scrutetur Iberos.
> Plus habet hic vitae, plus habet ille viae.

Let the other wander and scrutinize the
    outlandish Australians.
This one has more of God, that one has
    more of the road.

Here is demanded the eye and the nerve. Only the
defeated and deserters go to the wars—Cowards that
run away and enlist. O ye Chivalry, ye could not
fight a duel with your lives, and so ye challenged a
man!

I met a pilgrim travel-worn, who could speak all
tongues and conform himself to the customs of all
nations;—who carried a passport to all countries, and
was naturalized in all climes, who had vanquished
all the chimeras and caused the Sphinx to go and
dash her head against a stone—who never retraced
his steps nor returned to his native land, and was
reputed to have travelled further than all the travellers. He bore for device on his shield these words
only—"Know Thyself."

"Direct your eye sight inward, and you'll find
    A thousand regions in your mind
Yet undiscovered. Travel them, and be
    Expert in home-cosmographie."

Most revolutions in society have not power to interest, still less alarm us, but tell me that our rivers are
drying up, or the genus pine dying out in the country, and I might attend. Some events in history are
more remarkable than important, like eclipses of the
sun by which all are attracted, but whose effects no
one takes the trouble to calculate. Revolutions are
never sudden. The most important is commonly some
silent and unobtrusive fact in history. In the year 449
three Saxon cyules arrived on the British coast. "Three
scipen gode comen mid than flode."

To the sick the doctors wisely recommend a change of air and scenery. Who chains me to this dull town?

There is this moment proposed to me every kind of life that men lead anywhere or at any time—or that imagination can paint. By another spring I may be a mail carrier in Peru, or a South African planter, or a Siberian exile, or a Greenland whaler, or a settler on the Columbia River—or a Canton merchant, or a soldier in Mexico, or a mackerel fisher off Cape Sable, or a Robinson Crusoe in the Pacific, or a silent navigator of any sea.

How many are now standing on the European coast whom another spring will find located on the Wisconsin or the Sacramento!

I can move away from public opinion, from government, from religion, from education, from society. Shall I be reckoned a rateable poll in the county of Middlesex, or be rated at one spear under the palm trees of Guinea? Shall I raise corn and potatoes in Massachusetts, or figs and olives in Asia Minor? Sit out the day in my office in State street, or ride it out on the steppes of Tartary? For my Brobdingnag I may sail to Patagonia, for my Lilliput to Lapland. In Arabia and Persia my days' adventures may surpass the Arabian Nights entertainments. I may be a logger on the head waters of the Penobscot, to be recorded in fable hereafter as an amphibious river God by as sounding a name as Triton or Proteus.—Carry furs from Nootka to China and so be more renowned than Jason and his Golden Fleece, or join a South Sea exploring expedition to be recounted hereafter along with the Periplus of Hanno.

And how many more things may I do with which there is none to be compared!

Thank Heaven here is not all the world. The buckeye does not grow in New England, and the mocking bird is rarely heard here. Why should I fall behind the summer and the migrations of birds? Shall we not compete with the buffalo who keeps pace with the seasons, cropping the pastures of the Colorado till a greener and sweeter grass awaits him by the Yellowstone? The wild-goose is more a cosmopolite than we, —he breaks his fast in Canada—takes a luncheon in the Susquehanna, and plumes himself for the night in a Louisiana bayou. The pigeon carries an acorn in his crop from the King of Holland's to Mason and Dixon's Line. Yet we think if rail-fences are pulled down and stone walls set up on our farms, bounds are henceforth set to our lives and our fates decided. If you are chosen town-clerk forsooth, you cannot go to Tierra del Fuego this summer.

But what would all this activity amount to—?

> Goosey goosey gander
> Where shall I wander?
> Up stairs down stairs
> In a lady's chamber?

Shall we not stretch our legs?—Why shall we pause this side of sundown? We will not then be immigrants still further into our native country. Let us start now on that fartherest western way which does not pause at the Mississippi or the Pacific, pushing on by day and night, sun down—moon down—stars down—and at last earth down too.

Index

Rome, 138, 175
Rondont, 194

Sackets Harbor, 194
San Francisco, 163
Satan, 46
Saxon invasion of England,
 195
sculpture, the self as, 16-17
sea, private, 194
Second-Advent Tabernacle,
 52
"Service, The," 3-17
Shakespeare, quoted, 12, 66
Sharps' rifles, 127, 133, 152
Sheep's-Head Gully, 165
silence, 190
Simms, [Thomas], tragedy
 of, 93, 100, 101
slave, friends of dismayed,
 97; fugitive, 76, 93; held
 in Boston, 92; kissed by
 John Brown, 152; of United
 States President, 55
slaveholder, 132
slaveholders, 149
slaveholding mob, 149
"Slavery in Massachusetts,"
 91-109
slavery, 102, 108, 120, 129,
 132, 135, 138, 177;
 American ignorance of, 96;
 Anthony Burns returned to,
 106; constitutional sanction of, 87-88; effect of on
 John Brown, 124; ineffectual opposition to of mere
 opinion, 69; legions of,
 119; of newspapers, 101;
 passiveness as support of,
 71; produces no flower,
 109; proposal to lecture on,
 155; relation to Constitution of, 98; Webster on,
 87-88
slaves, 68; education worthy
 of, 151; fugitive, 95; futile
 attempts to rescue, 147;

government of, 67; in
 United States, 130
slave-ship, 124
sliding up hill, 103-04
social movements, 42
society, 187; annihilated by
 truth, 188
soldier, 71; a perfect
 machine, 119; brave, 14;
 serves state, 94
soul, as stern master, 14
"Soul's Errand, The," 140
South, 138, 147; opponents
 to reform in, 68
Southerners, 114
speech, simple and necessary,
 189
sphere, qualities of, 6-7
Sphinx, 195
Squire Make-a-Stir, 182
Stark, [John], 113
State, as half-witted, 80;
 as untrustworthy, 83; chief
 want in, 177; confronts
 only a man's body, 80;
 corrupt, man dangerous to,
 77; does not reward genius,
 158; how men serve the,
 66; ideal, imagined, 90;
 individual above, 89;
 interrupts lawful business,
 107; means of correcting
 injustice of, 74; refusal
 of allegiance to, 79, 84,
 106; reliance on protection
 of, 78; slaveholding, 151;
 support of church of, 79;
 taxes to, 73; thoughts
 murder toward, 108; union
 between self and, 72
steadfastness, need for, 15
Stevens, [Aaron], 128
Stollmeyer, C. F., 43
Sulky Gully, 164
sun, power of, 30-31; stored,
 33
Supreme Court, 98
surveying, ways of, 158